4.50
cat

05-186-5 (116811-5)

RUMANIA

Russia's Dissident Ally

RUMANIA

Russia's Dissident Ally

David Floyd

FREDERICK A. PRAEGER, *Publishers*
New York • Washington • London

FREDERICK A. PRAEGER, *Publishers*
111 Fourth Avenue, New York 3, N.Y., U.S.A.
77–79 Charlotte Street, London W.1, England

Published in the United States of America in 1965
by Frederick A. Praeger, Inc., Publishers

Library of Congress Catalog Card Number: 65-18077

This book is Number 160 in the series
Praeger Publications in Russian History and World Communism

Printed in the United States of America

Contents

Introduction

TOWARDS the end of 1963 there were rumours circulating in eastern Europe that Nikita Khrushchev, then first secretary of the Soviet Communist Party and prime minister of the USSR, had paid a secret visit to Rumania for the purpose of removing Gheorghe Gheorghiu-Dej, the leader of the Rumanian communist regime, and of cutting Rumania and the Rumanian communists down to size. The Rumanians themselves did nothing to refute these unconfirmable stories or to counteract the obvious conclusion that, if Khrushchev had indeed tried to impose his will on the party and government in power in Bucharest, he had failed.

His failure was the result of a long process of change in the relations between Bucharest and Moscow: change which had in fact gone so far by the end of 1963 that there was no question any longer that Khrushchev, or indeed any other Russian leader, could dictate to the Rumanians how they should conduct their affairs. The extent of the change was demonstrated in October 1964, when it was Khrushchev, and not Gheorghiu-Dej, who was removed from power. One of the many reasons given for the Soviet leader's downfall was his mishandling of Russia's relations with the countries of eastern Europe, and in particular with Rumania. Gheorghiu-Dej and his colleagues in the leadership of the Rumanian Communist Party could be forgiven if, in private at least, they gave themselves some of the credit for Khrushchev's removal.

In 1963, however, very few observers of the communist world realised how far the Rumanian regime had moved towards autonomy. For the world at large the Rumanian government was still a meek 'satellite' of the Soviet Union which had shown far less tendency to resist Russian control than had, for example, the governments of Poland or Hungary. But this was because the Rumanian 'revolt' had been conducted in a more sophisticated manner than the Polish or Hungarian revolts. For this reason it had been more and not less effective in extracting Rumania from the Russian embrace. It was a measure of Rumanian caution and tact that only in 1964 did the world at large become aware of the extent of the changes in Rumania's relations with Russia.

In the third week of April 1964, the members of the Central Committee of the Rumanian Workers' (Communist) Party were assembled in Bucharest, along with senior officials from every branch of the country's administration and economy, to hear and approve the views of the party's leaders on the state of relations between the countries in the communist world. Some days after the meeting, on April 27, the party published the text of the resolution approved by the Central Committee. It was entitled *A Statement on the Stand of the Rumanian Workers' Party concerning the Problems of the World Communist and Working-Class Movement*. This somewhat forbidding title concealed what was in effect the Rumanian communists' declaration of independence and an outright challenge to Moscow's authority in the communist world. It has remained the basic statement of principle upon which all the Rumanian leaders' subsequent moves in domestic and foreign policy have been founded.

At first reading, the *Statement* appeared to be primarily concerned with the dispute, then at its height, between the Russian and Chinese communists in which the Rumanian leaders had elected in March 1964 to assume the role of intermediaries. The beginning of the *Statement* contained an account of the Rumanians' efforts to halt Sino-Soviet polemics and of the journey made by the Rumanian prime minister, Ion Gheorghe Maurer, to China, North Korea and the Crimea, where he had seen Khrushchev. The latter part of the *Statement* contained an urgent appeal to all communist parties, and especially the Russian and Chinese parties, to resolve their differences and bend their efforts to avoid a split in the communist movement.

Sandwiched between these two sections—which were presumably intended to emphasise the Rumanian communists' devotion to the cause of communist unity—was a far more important section dealing with economic relations between communist states and in particular with certain important issues which had been raised within the Council for Mutual Economic Aid, the organisation linking the Soviet Union and the communist countries of eastern Europe, known in the non-communist world as 'Comecon'.

The *Statement* recalled that proposals had been put forward within Comecon for 'a joint plan and a single planning body for all member countries, interstate technical-productive branch unions, enterprises jointly owned by several countries, interstate economic complexes, and so forth'. On these proposals, the *Statement* said: 'our Party has expressed its point of view very clearly', and it went on to set these views out in plain language:

> ... since the essence of the suggested measures lies in shifting some functions of economic management from the competence of the State concerned to the competence of super-State bodies or organisms, *these measures are not in keeping with the principles underlying relations between socialist countries.*
>
> *The idea of a single planning body for all Comecon countries has the most serious economic and political implications.* The planned management of the national economy is one of the fundamental, essential and inalienable attributes of the sovereignty of the socialist State—the State plan being the principal means by which the socialist State achieves its political and socio-economic objectives, establishes the direction and rates of development of the national economy, its basic proportions, the accumulations and the measures for raising the people's living standard and cultural level. The sovereignty of the socialist State requires that it takes full and effective advantage of these means and retains in its hands all the levers for the management of economic and social life.
>
> *To hand over these levers to the competence of some super-State or extra-State bodies would be to turn sovereignty into a concept without any real content.*
>
> All this applies equally to inter-State technical-productive

ix

branch unions, as well as enterprises commonly owned by two or several States. The State Plan is one and indivisible, and no parts or sections can be separated from it to be transferred outside the State. The management of the national economy as a whole is not possible if the questions of managing some branches or enterprises are taken out of the competence of the Party and Government of a particular country and transferred to extra-State bodies.

This was, on the face of it, scarcely the language of revolt. To the uninitiated, indeed, these words might appear to be no more than a rather humdrum restatement of principles which have long been common currency in the civilised world. But in the context of relations between the countries of the communist world, and between Rumania and the Soviet Union in particular, as they stood in the spring of 1964, the Rumanian *Statement* was in fact a clear act of defiance of Moscow and of Khrushchev. It marked the end of a Russian effort to bring eastern Europe under control by economic, as distinct from political and military, means.

The significance of the passages in the *Statement* quoted above becomes clearer if it is recalled that the author of the proposals for closer integration in Comecon and the creation of supranational bodies was Khrushchev himself. It was he who in August 1962 had put his name to an article published in the September issue of *Kommunist*—the Soviet Communist Party's principal and most authoritative political journal—and later reproduced in *Problems of Peace and Socialism*, the journal of the international communist movement.* The appearance of the article followed closely on a major 'summit' meeting in Moscow of the leaders of all the Comecon member countries summoned to discuss the problem of injecting new life into the moribund Comecon organisation. There was no mistaking the fact—both because of the importance of its author and because of the great prominence it was given—that Khrushchev's article represented a major departure in Soviet policy towards the countries of eastern Europe, and one to which the Russians attached considerable importance.

The communist countries had arrived at a state, Khrushchev said,

* Published in English as the *World Marxist Review*.

when conditions have ripened for raising their economic and political co-operation to a new and higher level. At this level a special significance is acquired by co-ordinated national-economic plans, the socialist international division of labour and by the co-ordination and specialisation of production which will guarantee the successful organic development of the socialist countries.

What Khrushchev called the 'socialist world system' had reached the stage where, he said, 'it is no longer possible to chart its development correctly by simply adding up the national economies'. The time had come to advance towards 'that single world-wide organism embracing the system as a whole which Lenin's genius foresaw'.

It was now possible, Khrushchev said, for the communist countries to engage in planning at the level of Comecon. *'Our aim is to build the socialist world economy as a single entity.'* If they had not been able to do so in the past, it was because under its old statute Comecon did not have the necessary powers or the necessary 'planning instruments'. But this had now been corrected and, Khrushchev said, 'the decisions of the June meeting will enable the work of the Council to be organised in a new way'.

Khrushchev was overoptimistic. However attractive and logical his proposals might appear to the planners in the Kremlin, they raised many anxious questions in the minds of the men—at least of some of the men—who ruled the countries of eastern Europe. There followed in 1963 a series of stormy meetings of Comecon's Executive Committee and, in July 1963, a meeting of all the party leaders of eastern Europe at which Khrushchev and his plans for economic integration were in effect defeated. Comecon did not receive the 'necessary powers' or the 'planning instruments' which Khrushchev promised, and by the end of 1964 it seemed highly improbable that his ill-thought-out scheme for making a 'single entity' of the Soviet and Eastern Bloc economies would ever be realised. With Khrushchev himself removed from the scene, his successors had to seek other means of holding Russia's east European empire together.

Little is known of the actual debates that went on behind the closed doors of the Comecon meetings in 1962 and 1963. But there is no doubt that the revolt against the Khrushchev plan was led by the Rumanians and that, whatever support they enjoyed from the other east European communists, their firm opposition to the plans for integration was sufficient to wreck them. The *Statement* approved and published by the Rumanian Central Committee in April 1964 was not only a declaration of independence but also a proclamation of victory.

April 1964 also saw the celebration of Khrushchev's seventieth birthday. It was an occasion which Gheorghiu-Dej found it impossible to attend. The Rumanian government, however, conferred upon Khrushchev Rumania's highest honour: the Star of Rumania. It was small compensation for Rumania's obstinate opposition to his policies. But in 1964 the Rumanian leaders seemed no longer to attach much importance to Khrushchev and his downfall in October seemed to come as no surprise to them.

At first sight, the Rumanian communists' resistance to Soviet controls would scarcely bear comparison with Marshal Tito's spectacular defiance of Stalin in 1948, with the Hungarian people's revolt against Russian domination in 1956, or even with the reaction against stalinism in Poland in the same year. The Rumanian action was conducted with the greatest discretion and the minimum of public recrimination and throughout in the name of unity. Yet for all that it was none the less effective. Indeed, by 1965 Rumania was no less free of Russian control than was Jugoslavia, which had shaken off the trammels of the Kremlin in 1948, and Rumania's leaders were pursuing a far more independent, original line of policy in their foreign relations than either Kadar in Hungary or Gomulka in Poland. Though the Hungarian people, despite the brutal suppression of their revolt in 1956, had subsequently gained a great deal in terms of internal ease and relaxation, their communist rulers appeared nervous in their policy-making and ever conscious of the force that had installed them in the seat of power. And the Polish people, who had shown such unwonted self-control in 1956, had seen their reward in the steady whittling away of their gains by a leader who appeared to be utterly unaware of his potential power and freedom of manoeuvre.

By the end of 1964, while the Rumanian leaders were bursting with self-confidence and obviously enjoying the success of their economic policies at home and abroad, a mood of deep depression had settled on most of the other communist capitals of eastern Europe.

This book sets out to tell the story of the Rumanian 'revolt', to examine its origins and roots in the past, and to consider its significance for the rest of eastern Europe and Russia's relations with its European neighbours.

On March 19, 1965, Gheorghe Gheorghiu-Dej died, at the age of 63. He was accorded a state funeral on March 24, which was attended by both President Anastas Mikoyan of the USSR and the Chinese prime minister, Chou En-lai. Even before Gheorghiu-Dej was laid to rest the Central Committee of the Rumanian Communist Party met to decide on the succession. His position as first secretary of the party was given to Nicolae Ceausescu, the 46-year-old member of the Politburo who had in fact long been acting as first secretary under Gheorghiu-Dej's general supervision. A Rumanian of peasant stock, Ceausescu became a communist in his youth and was leader of the communist youth organization in Rumania before the second world war. He spent the war years in Rumania, and in 1945, at the age of 27, he was appointed secretary of the Bucharest party organisation. He subsequently became deputy minister of Agriculture (in 1949) and deputy minister for the Armed Forces (in 1950). In 1954 Ceausescu was made a secretary of the Central Committee of the Rumanian Communist Party, and in 1955 he was raised to full membership in the Politburo. He is above all an 'organisation man'—a professional party official who in the latter years of Gheorghiu-Dej's life was the effective controller of the party machine.

Gheorghiu-Dej's other post, as chairman of the State Council and head of state, was given to his old friend and ally, Chivu Stoica, who had served from 1955 to 1961 as prime minister but who had since then occupied only posts in the Politburo and secretariat of the party. The man who had succeeded him as prime minister and had been in the forefront of Rumania's campaign to carve a new position in the world, Ion Gheorghe Maurer, remained at the head of the government.

These were not radical or surprising changes. They meant that Ceausescu had acquired, in addition to the duties of first secretary, the full authority of the title as well. But he did not succeed to the largely honorific post as head of state, and this was a measure of his lesser prestige and authority in Rumanian political life. It remained to be seen whether he would eventually be able to assert his authority over his colleagues, some of whom were a good deal older and more experienced and possibly cleverer than he.

But there was no reason to expect sharp conflicts among the surviving leaders of the Rumanian Communist Party in the near future nor any deviation from the general line of policy laid down in the last few years. They had all worked together for many years; they had jointly resisted Russian pressures; and they had had the satisfaction of seeing their policies succeed. Moreover, Ceausescu was considered to be even more of a 'Rumania-firster' than Gheorghiu-Dej, and he was unlikely to come to blows with Maurer. They appeared to have every interest in maintaining a united front both to the East and to the West.

It was the loss of Gheorghiu-Dej's shrewd political instinct that would be the most difficult to overcome, because no amount of experience or technical skill is a substitute for the sort of political qualities that Gheorghiu-Dej had. He had made himself undisputed leader of Rumanian communism and of the Rumanian state against heavy odds and ruthless rivals and in a world where politics is a more than usually rough game to play. He had steered Rumania out from under Russian control and into a state of relative independence with consummate skill, never allowing the process to get out of hand. There must have been many occasions when his shrewdness and wisdom acted as a brake on the enthusiasm of his colleagues. What would they do now that the brake was off?

1

The Land and the People

Romînul nu piere (The Rumanian never dies)—proverb.

THOUGH Bucharest is today only a few hours by air from the capitals of western Europe, Rumania remains an almost unknown country and few people are aware of what sort of people the Rumanians are, what language they speak, or what relations they bear to their neighbours in the Balkans. This is scarcely surprising if we recall that, before the second world war and the advent of air travel, Rumania was a very remote land indeed. Almost all the brave souls who did venture so far afield by motor car or train found it worth their while to record their impressions and their adventures in a book. Anyone who visits a good library in search of information about Rumania will find these volumes with their quaint illustrations stacked on the shelves. They constitute most of the outside world's knowledge of Rumania.

Then, from 1940, Rumania was cut off from the rest of the world by the German occupation and the conditions of war. When the war ended, Rumania was released from nazi domination only to fall immediately under Russian control. The 'iron curtain' quickly came down across Europe and Rumania became even more remote from western Europe in the middle of the twentieth century than it had been between the wars. It is only

1

in the last few years that the Rumanian government has opened its doors to a regular flow of visitors, mainly businessmen and tourists from the West. It is small wonder, then, that few people have any idea of who or what the Rumanians are. For the man in the street they are probably just another of those strange peoples of eastern Europe, related in some way to the Russians, who have for reasons best known to themselves adopted the communist system of government.

Yet one has only to spend a few days in Rumania to sense at once the wide differences between the Rumanians and the peoples—mainly Slavs—who surround them. You do not need to be told that the Rumanians are *not* Slavs, like their neighbours—the Russians, Ukrainians, Serbs and Croats. It is amply evident from their appearance and their bearing. It is even more apparent when you come to speak or read their language. Indeed, when, in the spring and summer of 1964, I drove around the Rumanian countryside, wandered round the streets of Bucharest, talked to Rumanians in their homes and restaurants, and tried to puzzle out exactly why it was the Rumanians who had stood up to the Russians, I was forced back time and time again to the simple fact of their national and racial distinction from the Russians. Not, of course, that the simple fact of being Slav necessarily makes a nation either pro-Russian or pro-communist. But the Rumanian antipathy to Russia and communism seems to go much deeper than it does in the case, say, of the Czechs. There is in the Rumanians as a whole nothing that draws them eastwards to Moscow.

What, then, is Rumania, and who are the Rumanian people? We must study a few basic facts before we can understand the latest stage in the troubled history of Rumania's relations with Russia.

Rumania is a country in the south-east corner of Europe, in what we have come to know as the Balkans. Within its present somewhat truncated boundaries it covers an area of nearly 92,000 square miles, which is almost the same as the area of the United Kingdom. It is rather larger than the state of Minnesota, but smaller than Colorado. Its population today (1965) is close to the 19 million mark—roughly the same as Jugoslavia's.

Rumania is surrounded by other communist states, albeit one of them is the equally dissident Jugoslavia. The others are the Soviet Union—with which it has a common frontier of 825 miles—Hungary and Bulgaria. In addition, Rumania has a 150-mile coastline on the Black Sea. Today the problem of access to the West is no longer important, but in the early post-war years, especially when Jugoslavia was also a loyal ally of Moscow, the fact that Rumania was completely cut off from western Europe certainly limited the Rumanian's possibilities of manoeuvre.

Rumania is a mountainous country, with over a third of its territory lying too high to be of use for cultivation. Far from forming a natural boundary for the Rumanian state, the mountain ranges—the eastern, southern and western Carpathians—tend to divide the country into distinct areas. Between the Transylvanian Alps, which run east-west across the country, and the river Danube, which forms Rumania's southern frontier with Bulgaria, are lowlands, known in history as Wallachia. Here we find the capital, Bucharest, and many of the country's more important industrial cities, notably Ploesti, one of the centres of the Rumanian oil industry.

At their eastern end, the Transylvanian Alps curve round in a right-angle and turn northwards to form the southern section of the main Carpathian mountain mass, leaving another area of plain between the highland and the present eastern frontier with Russia. This is Moldavia, where agriculture is more important than industry. On the western side of the mountains, between the right-angle and the Hungarian frontier to the north-west, is the plateau of Transylvania, which contains the greater part of Rumania's rich mineral resources. Stretching westward from the Transylvanian Alps towards Hungary and northern Jugoslavia, and merging into the great Danubian plain, is the Banat, a rich agricultural area. For a country of its size, Rumania has an extraordinary variety of physical structure and scenery.

Until a program of intensive industrialisation was initiated by the communist regime in the post-war period, Rumania was primarily an agricultural country. Before the second world war, only a fifth of the population lived in towns, and even today two thirds of the people still live in the countryside and are engaged in agriculture. Rich, fertile soils and an equable climate made Rumania one of Europe's largest producers of grain, of which it exported large quantities between

3

the wars. But the Rumanian countryside has suffered from over-population and the consequent parcelling out of the land, and from the lack of capital investment. Rumania's vast reserves of timber have never been properly exploited.

More important for the country's economic advance in the modern world are the considerable natural resources hidden beneath the ground. Rumania has the largest resources of oil and natural gas of any country in Europe and is among the richest countries of Europe in deposits of bauxite. It has important deposits of coal, manganese and iron ore—though not of very high quality—together with some copper, lead and zinc, and is one of Europe's few producers of uranium and other radioactive materials. Finally, but by no means least important as a source of economic independence, Rumania has long been a producer of gold and silver.

In terms of natural resources, therefore, Rumania is among the best endowed nations of Europe and potentially richer than any other of Russia's allies in eastern Europe. The awareness of their undeveloped resources and potential wealth has played an important part in encouraging and enabling the Rumanians to assert themselves in recent years.

About 85 per cent of Rumania's population, over 16 million people, consists of Rumanians proper. The rest of the population is made up of various minority peoples, of whom the Hungarians and the Germans are the most important.

Who are the Rumanians? The emergence of a distinct Rumanian people is believed to have been the result of the Emperor Trajan's occupation in the second century AD of the kingdom of Dacia, which covered roughly the whole of the territory between the Danube and the Dniester today occupied by Rumania. The Roman legions remained in the area until the end of the third century, imposing their language and culture on the Dacian people whom they appear in the end to have completely assimilated.

But the thousand years following the withdrawal of the Roman legions was truly a 'dark age' for the Daco-Roman, or Rumanian, people. Invaders from the east swept across their territory again and again, dispersing settled communities, forcing them to flee either northwards into the mountains or southwards

4

across the Danube, and destroying all record of their social life.

The Rumanian people do not reappear in written history until the twelfth century and their modern history begins with the formation in the thirteenth and fourteenth centuries of the Rumanian principalities of Wallachia and Moldavia. These Christian states, based on a feudal social system, came under Turkish domination at the turn of the fifteenth century. The Turks did not, however, conquer Wallachia and Moldavia as they had Serbia and Bulgaria, but imposed suzerainty and exacted tribute through the native princes and the landed nobility (boyars). One of the main results of this exploitation was a long period of economic and social stagnation and the steady impoverishment of the Rumanian peasantry.

An even more disastrous period of Rumanian history followed when, at the beginning of the eighteenth century, the Rumanian princes and boyars were replaced by the Phanariots: Greek merchants from Constantinople whose sole function was to exploit the territories and the people they ruled for the benefit of themselves and their Turkish masters. For another century Rumania stood still, as far as economic or social progress was concerned. But it did not stand still politically, and the early part of the nineteenth century saw the spread of ideas originating in France and Greece which led eventually to the development of a powerful nationalist movement. The culminating episode in this movement was the restoration of Rumanian princes to the thrones of Moldavia and Wallachia in 1821.

The nineteenth century saw the rapid emergence of Rumania as a modern European state, the establishment of a native Rumanian dynasty and the development of relations with the great powers of Europe. By exploiting relations with Russia and France against the Turks, the United Principalities of Moldavia and Wallachia, henceforth to be known as Rumania, achieved autonomy in 1859. Then, as a result of the Russo-Turkish War, in which the Rumanian armies made an important contribution to the Russian victory, Rumania gained its independence, and was given international recognition as a sovereign state at the Congress of Berlin in 1878.

The friendship of the great powers for Rumania was not entirely disinterested. Rumania was regarded, especially by Russia, as a valuable bulwark against Turkish ambitions. Indeed, imperial Russia came to regard Rumania as its natural sphere of influence, at times exercising complete control over the country's life—not always in an unenlightened manner. But, with the granting of independence and with closer economic and cultural links with western Europe—with France in particular—the Rumanian state embarked on a period of rapid economic expansion and political progress, which was delayed but not halted by the first world war. Indeed, Rumania's decision to enter the war on the side of the Entente powers and against Austria and Germany was largely governed by its leaders' aspirations for a 'Greater Rumania'.

This ambition was achieved at the end of the war, which cost Rumania a tenth of its population, then only seven million. The collapse of the Austro-Hungarian empire and the overthrow of the tsarist regime in Russia made it possible for the first time to unite under one rule practically everybody who could claim to be Rumanian. Under the Versailles settlement, Rumania was given Transylvania (which had been almost continuously in the possession of the Hungarians since the eleventh century), the Bukovina (which had been lost to Austria in 1775), Bessarabia (which Russia had annexed in 1812), and the Banat (which had also belonged to Austria). Thus at one stroke of the pen the area and the population of the kingdom of Rumania were doubled: an achievement undoubtedly very gratifying to Rumanian patriots. But the speed at which this new unity had been achieved tended to obscure the difficulties besetting the formation of a new state. Not the least of these was the fact that a quarter of the population of the new Rumania now consisted of non-Rumanian national minorities.

Having thus satisfied their immediate ambitions, Rumania's rulers, first under King Ferdinand and later under his son King Carol II, pursued a foreign policy aimed at preserving its integrity and security. This policy was based on alliances with the Western Powers, primarily Britain and France, on support of the League of Nations, and on regional alliances, known as the Little Entente and the Balkan Entente. It was not unreasonable for a small and backward country in south-eastern Europe to seek safety in numbers, and Rumania had the good fortune to have a statesman of European stature, in the person of Nicolae Titulescu, in command of its foreign affairs until 1936.

It was also not entirely unreasonable for the Rumanian rulers' main preoccupation to be with the possibility of encroachments from the east rather than with the threat of aggression by Germany from the west. But it was Hitler and not Stalin who came to dominate European and therefore Rumanian political life in the 'thirties. In the face of growing internal problems, accentuated by the economic crisis that enveloped Europe, King Carol in 1936 assumed dictatorial powers and came to rely on the reactionary 'Iron Guard' movement which drew inspiration from Hitler's Germany. As Hitler's grip on Europe grew stronger and the influence of Britain and France receded, Rumania fell increasingly under German domination.

Yet it was not the Germans but the Russians who were the first to take advantage of Rumania's isolation from its traditional allies. By 1939, it is true, the Rumanian economy was almost entirely at the service of the German war machine. But Rumania was still intact and as independent as any country could be in Hitler's Europe. On August 23, 1939, however, Stalin concluded his infamous pact with Hitler: the agreement which made the outbreak of the second world war inevitable. Attached to this treaty was a 'Secret Additional Protocol' which recorded the way the Russians and Germans regarded their respective spheres of influence in eastern Europe. The Baltic states were to fall to Russia, Poland was to be divided between the two of them, and:

3. With regard to south-eastern Europe, attention is called by the Soviet side to its interest in Bessarabia. The German side declares its complete political disinterestedness in these areas.

Thus Stalin obtained Hitler's 'all clear' for his eventual annexation of Bessarabia.

Russian 'interest' in Bessarabia had revived very quickly after the bolshevik seizure of power in 1917. By 1924 the Soviet government was already demanding a plebiscite in the area and the Russians' insistence on recovering what had belonged to the Tsar continued until 1934 to prevent the establishment of normal relations between Rumania and the Soviet Union. When at last the two governments recognised each other, the status of Bessarabia was not mentioned, and this was regarded by the

Rumanians as Russian acceptance of the Rumanian claim to the territory.

But, as the secret protocol to the Russo-German Pact showed, the dream of reacquiring Bessarabia and the northern Bukovina never left the Russian mind, and it was not long after receiving Hitler's acquiesence in this ambition that the Soviet government began to put renewed pressure on the Rumanians. By June 1940 they were ready to move in. On June 25, Molotov, the Soviet foreign minister, was telling the Italian ambassador in Moscow that: 'The Soviet Union would prefer to realise its claims to Bessarabia without war, but, if that were impossible because of Rumanian intransigence, it was determined to resort to force.'

The next day Molotov summoned the Rumanian minister in Moscow and informed him that the Soviet government demanded the immediate cession of Bessarabia and the northern Bukovina. At the same time as it received this ultimatum, the Rumanian government also received a message from the German foreign minister, von Ribbentrop, advising the Rumanians to accede to the Russian demand 'in order to avoid war between Rumania and the Soviet Union'. On June 28, without acknowledging any Russian rights to Bessarabia, the Rumanian government—lacking the slightest support from allies near or far—did the only thing it could do and yielded to the Russian demand. Within a few days, the Red Army had swept across Bessarabia and established itself on the river Prut.

The Russians offered no 'ideological' arguments for their reannexation of Bessarabia. In their negotiations with the Germans they spoke simply as a great power of their 'interest' in the region. It may be presumed that this interest was at the time partly strategic and possibly intended to improve the Soviet position in the event of a war with Germany which seemed, at least to some, to be inevitable. But it seems primarily to have been another instance of pure Russian expansionism and was undoubtedly so regarded by the great majority of Rumanians.

The Russian action was the signal for both the Hungarians and the Bulgarians to step in and take advantage of Rumania's plight and of German compliance. Hungary took about 16,000 square miles of Transylvania with over two and a half million people, half of whom were Rumanians, while Bulgaria seized the southern Dobrogea. The kingdom of Rumania lost a third of its territory and population in three swift blows, and popular reaction was so strong that King Carol was forced to abdicate.

Thus, only some twenty years after they had achieved their Greater Rumania, the Rumanian people were forced to see it dismembered and carved up amongst their neighbours. Those of us who live behind more settled frontiers should reflect not only on the bitter hatred that such treatment must engender between peoples but on the moral effect it must have upon a whole nation. Such disruption and disorganisation, added to the effects of war, demoralised the Rumanian nation and stultified its political and economic life. It must be difficult for any Rumanian, whether he is nominally a communist or not, to forget that it was the Russians, in alliance with the Germans, who tore his nation apart.

The visitor to Rumania may often be surprised today by the violence of patriotic emotion expressed by Rumanians in private conversations—the authorities still hesitate, and wisely, to give open encouragement to such sentiments. But the surprise is less if one recalls what Rumania has suffered at the hands of its neighbours. No Rumanian ruler who wishes to establish friendly relations between his people and the Russians, Hungarians, Bulgars and Jugoslavs has an enviable job.

The Russian occupation of Bessarabia lasted on this occasion only as long as the Russo-German Pact held good: just a year. On June 22, 1941, Hitler launched his grand assault on Russia. On the same day, Rumanian divisions, under the direct command of General Ion Antonescu—the virtual dictator of the country under the young King Michael—crossed the river Prut and quickly established themselves on the Dniester, thus reuniting Bessarabia with Rumania. The Rumanians were avenged on the Russians.

But, carried away, no doubt, by the ease with which he had liberated the 'lost provinces' and by the speed of the German advance along the whole front, Antonescu decided to push his armies across the Dniester and further into Russia. What had begun as a campaign to restore to Rumania territory to which it had a legitimate claim then became a piece of undisguised

9

Rumanian expansionism. Antonescu was taking advantage of Russia's initial defeats to seize territory to which Rumania had no claim. The Rumanians occupied an area of some 10,000 square miles extending up to the river Bug and including the city of Odessa which was made the capital and headquarters of the Rumanian administration. When the tide of war on the eastern front turned, it became quickly apparent that Antonescu had grossly over-reached himself: a mistake for which the Rumanian people had to pay dearly both in casualties and in loss of territory. It would be too much to suggest that, if Antonescu had not gone beyond the Dniester, the Russians would later have respected Rumania's frontier on the Prut. But it is possible that, in the uncertain situation prevailing towards the end of the war, they would have been less inclined to seize Bessarabia as un-ceremoniously as they did if the Rumanians themselves had not advanced so far into Soviet territory during the war. At all events the episode did nothing to improve relations between Russians and Rumanians, and it appeared to provide some excuse for Russian suspicions of Rumanian motives and for Soviet punitive actions against Rumania after the war.

Even this brief glance at how the Rumanian people came into being and to occupy the territory in south-east Europe where they are today makes clear their extraordinary resilience and capacity to preserve their identity through centuries of foreign rule and abuse. It seems almost a miracle that so small, backward and relatively defenceless a people should have been able to survive and to preserve a distinct national culture. But they *have* survived, and there they are, to be seen in the streets of Bucharest and in the villages of the Rumanian countryside: dark-haired, sallow-skinned and unmistakably Latin in their appearance and behaviour. And there, for any doubters to read and hear, is their language, overwhelmingly Latin in vocabulary and structure, but with sufficient traces of Slavonic and Turkish influence to remind us of Rumania's troubled history. Sir Charles Petrie has attributed the strength of the Rumanians' national consciousness primarily to their racial origins. 'It is in the memory of imperial Rome that the Rumanians have for generations sought their inspiration.' They had survived as a national entity, he says, 'very largely owing to this belief in a Latin origin which separated them from and culturally raised them above their conquerers of the moment'.*

A nation that has survived such vicissitudes on what has been for centuries one of the main crossroads of Europe must certainly have within it a strength of national spirit and pride which needs no artificial stimuli and which must be one of the most powerful factors influencing the policy of anyone who tries to rule Rumania. Nationalism—and not necessarily nationalism in its worst sense—flourishes in the Balkans with a vigour and a fire that surprises people who have grown up in regions where national rivalries and ambitions have subsided. More than once I have been amazed and even embarrassed at the violence which an ordinary Rumanian can inject into his discussion of national issues. We may deplore this; but we should nevertheless remember that such a spirit is an indispensable factor in national survival.

It is also clear that the Rumanians have learnt through history, not only how to resist and repel the invader and would-be occupier, but also how to bend with the wind and accept foreign rule when it seemed unavoidable. They have learnt how to preserve their national identity and traditions even within the limits imposed by alien domination. And they also have long experience of working slowly and patiently to rid themselves of unwanted masters. Perhaps I exaggerate; perhaps it is an illusion to imagine that peoples as a whole can store up their experience and learn from the past. And yet, too much of Rumanian history seems to have been re-enacted in the last ten years for it to be altogether accidental.

Apart from the positive force of nationalism, there is also the negative force of hostility to other nations and peoples. A people which has lived for centuries in a state of constant friction with many neighbours can scarcely be expected to learn to love them. When the price of maintaining a nation at all has been constant vigilance and suspicion, lasting friendship and alliances are unlikely to form. Ethnic and linguistic differences apart, there is no love lost between the Rumanians and the Russians, the Rumanians and the Hungarians, the Rumanians and the Bulgars, the Rumanians and the Serbs. They do not like each

* *The Quarterly Review*, April 1939. Quoted by Victor Cornea in *British Survey*, August 1957.

other, and nothing that has happened in the last twenty years has encouraged them to overcome their mutual antipathies.

The loss of Bessarabia to Russia at the end of the second world war did nothing to endear the Rumanians to the Russians. But the demands of 'proletarian internationalism' prevented these issues from being aired in the Rumanian press, and the Rumanian government insists today that it has no territorial disputes with any country—implying that it lays no claim to Bessarabia, but also that it will accept no demands on Transylvania from Hungary. Their extreme sensitivity in this matter was demonstrated most clearly in 1964, when the Rumanian authorities came across what they took to be a Russian plan for the further division of their territory. The violence of their reaction, which is described later (see below page 105), provided the outside world with a brief glimpse of the fires of nationalism burning in the Rumanian soul.

Rumania's relations with Hungary are bedevilled by the apparently insoluble problem of the large Hungarian minority in Transylvania. There are in Rumania about 1,800,000 people who regard themselves as Hungarian and speak Magyar, inhabiting mostly Transylvania and Crisana-Mures. They are the descendants of those Hungarians who occupied Transylvania (which the Rumanians claim to be their original home) in the eleventh century and remained in practically unchallenged possession of the area right down to this century, when, at the end of the first world war, it was handed over to the Rumanians. The existence of this large, alien and undigested community in the centre of their territory has been a constant problem for Rumania's rulers both between the wars and since the second world war. Though it is dormant today, the emotions aroused among the Hungarian minority by the popular revolt in Hungary in 1956 suggested that the problem is far from solution.

The only other minority group of any serious consequence consists of some 400,000 ethnic Germans—Saxons and Swabians, who were settled in Transylvania and the Banat by the Hapsburgs in the seventeenth century. Their numbers were sharply reduced by population transfers during the second world war, so that they do not constitute a problem comparable in any way with that presented by the Hungarians.

Rumania has within its boundaries many other ethnic

groups, ranging in size from a few thousands to some tens of thousands, which serve to remind us of the extent to which the country has been a crossroads of the peoples. There are Jews and Gypsies, Serbs and Croats, Russians and Ukrainians, Czechs and Slovaks, Turks and Tartars, Bulgarians, Greeks, Armenians and Poles. But none of these groups is large enough to represent a problem for Bucharest.

Such is the 'personality' of the people and the country which the Russian armies over-ran in 1944. This latest occupation of their territory was no milder than earlier invasions had been, and in many ways it was more oppressive and more complete in its grip on the country. Once again Rumania appeared to have been practically obliterated. But the forces which had preserved Rumania for centuries again came into action, though they had a long and difficult struggle ahead.

2

The Return of the Russians

How would it do for you to have ninety per cent predominance in Rumania . . .?—*Winston Churchill to
Joseph Stalin, October, 1944.*

BY the beginning of 1943, the prospects of a German victory,
on which Antonescu had based his plans, were fading. In February came the German surrender at Stalingrad, in which Rumanian troops suffered heavy losses, and by November the Russians were again in occupation of Kiev, capital of the Ukraine.
In the course of the year, the government in Bucharest began
to seek ways of coming to terms with the Western allies and of
withdrawing from the war. But it soon became clear that it
was the Russians and not the British or Americans who were
going to have the decisive word over the terms on which the
Rumanians were to be permitted to extricate themselves from
their unsuccessful alliance.

The Russian armies forced the Dniester in March 1944
and entered Rumanian territory proper in the first days of April.
Molotov, the Soviet foreign minister, immediately issued a re-
assuring statement that the Soviet government 'does not pursue
the aim of acquiring any part of Rumanian territory or of
changing the existing social order in Rumania'. The entry of
Soviet troops into Rumania was, he said, simply the result of the

14

military situation and the continued German resistance. Shortly after this statement was made, however, the Russians informed the Rumanians of their minimum demands for the conclusion of an armistice, for which they had already obtained the approval of the Western allies. The conditions were: a complete break with the Axis powers and co-operation with the Allies; the cession of Bessarabia and the northern Bukovina to Russia; the payment of reparations; and the repatriation of Allied prisoners. For their part, the Russians supported the restitution of northern Transylvania to Rumania and undertook to collaborate with Rumanian troops in its recovery: an undertaking which later proved to be something less than disinterested.

The Russians were in no hurry in the spring of 1944 to respond to the Rumanian approaches for an armistice which were being made in Cairo. They had no reason for haste, since the progress of the military campaign promised them the eventual occupation of Rumania in any case, and since Britain and the United States had already accepted the principle that the Russians were to handle Rumanian affairs on their own in the summer of 1944. But by August 1944, King Michael—who bore no responsibility for Rumania's entry into the war on the side of the Axis—and the leaders of the democratic opposition in Rumania had every reason for trying to swing their country over to the Allied side in the hope of saving it, even at that late moment, from being treated entirely as an enemy power.

The king and his advisers succeeded brilliantly in their first objective; but they failed in the second. Knowing that the Russians were about to launch their summer offensive, which was intended to carry their armies deep into the Balkans, the king decided to accept the armistice terms laid down by the Russians and to inform the Allies accordingly. On the morning of August 23, he summoned Marshal Antonescu to tell him of his decision and instruct him to take the necessary action. But, well aware that Antonescu would be unlikely to fall in easily with his plan, the young king had taken the precaution of strengthening the palace guard with units loyal to him and the democratic cause, and of having groups of Bucharest communists armed and installed in the palace. The latter were under the command of Emil Bodnaras, a former army officer who had turned communist, had lived for ten years in Russia, and had returned only in 1944 to organise communist resistance in Rumania. He is today a member of the Politburo of the Rumanian Workers' Party and a deputy prime minister.

Antonescu delayed responding to the king's summons until the evening and when he did appear it was to enter into heated argument over the king's proposal. Antonescu refused to despatch the telegram to the Allies in the form in which it had been drawn up and demanded an opportunity to contact the Germans. At this, the king accused him of intending to bargain with the Germans and told him he was under arrest. Soldiers entered and seized Marshal Antonescu. Two years later, after he had spent many painful months in Russian prisons, by which time his fears for Rumania's future were seen to be justified, Antonescu was put before a special tribunal in Bucharest and condemned to death. He met his death with great dignity.

Later, in the evening of August 23, King Michael spoke on Bucharest Radio to inform his people of his decision and of the formation of a new government headed by General Sanatescu and including representatives of the National Peasant Party (Iuliu Maniu), the Liberal Party (Bratianu), the Social-Democratic Party (C. Titel Petrescu) and the Communist Party (Lucretiu Patrascanu). The popular reaction, which expressed itself in wild demonstrations of enthusiasm in front of the royal palace, made it clear that the king had not misjudged the mood of his people. Subsequent events were to show, however, that he and his advisers had been overoptimistic about the reaction of the Western powers and the goodwill of the Russians.

The events of August 23, 1944, were later to be the subject of a variety of different interpretations. Nearly a year later, after the end of hostilities in June 1945, the Russians took the most unusual step of conferring on King Michael their Order of Victory: a distinction which they reserved for such outstanding military leaders as General Dwight Eisenhower, Field Marshal Montgomery and, indeed, Stalin himself. This unique decoration of a monarch by a communist state was presumably in recognition of the fact that the withdrawal of the Rumanian forces from the war had greatly speeded the Russian advance in southern Europe. It may also have reflected a Russian desire to be associated with a king who obviously enjoyed considerable popularity which Moscow might exploit for its own purposes.

It is unlikely that in August 1944 the Russians had a very clear idea of the political situation inside Rumania or of the forces upon which they would later have to rely for their control of the country. But they knew that their natural ally, the Rumanian Communist Party, was not strong. Though it had been in existence since 1921, it had never commanded a large following, and the arrest, during the fascist period in the mid-1930s, of practically all its leaders reduced the party to impotence. Then came Rumania's entry into the war on the side of the Germans and the social and economic upheavals that accompanied it, which made the organisation of communist activity practically impossible. Even if some kind of underground organisation remained in existence during the war years, it is doubtful whether there were more than a couple of thousand acknowledged communists in Rumania in 1944.

The leaders of the communist movement were not only in prison: they were divided into two distinct groups. One group, which came to be regarded as the 'native' group, consisted of those leaders who had remained in Rumania, mostly for the good and sufficient reason that they were held in Rumanian prisons or detention camps. The other group—the 'Muscovites' —consisted of those leaders who had spent the war years, or even longer, in Russia. Some of them had escaped to Russia from fascism before the war began, some had managed to make their way there during the war, and others had reached there through an exchange of prisoners between the Soviet and Rumanian governments in 1940. There appears to have been little contact maintained between these two groups of leaders in the war years, with the result that by 1944 their views on policy differed substantially.

Among the leaders who had stayed in Rumania were some who were still at liberty, the principal of whom were Foris, Koffler and Patrascanu. But their failure to have organised any effective underground activities caused them to be eyed with distrust both by those who were in prison and by those who were in Moscow. The better-known names among those in prison were: Gheorghe Gheorghiu-Dej, Gheorghe Apostol, Chivu Stoica, Alexandru Moghioros, Nicolae Ceausescu, Iosif Chisinevschi and Miron Constantinescu. All, with the exception of the latter two, still occupy leading posts in the communist regime today.

Gheorghe Gheorghiu-Dej was born in 1901 in the Moldavian town of Barlad. His father was a simple worker and he himself was obliged to earn his living from an early age. He became a skilled electrician and worked first at Galati, the Danubian port, and later on the Rumanian railways. He appears always to have played an active part in the trade union movement, but he did not join the communist movement until 1930. Before that date he appears to have been a member of the Social Democratic Party and even for a time of the National Peasant Party. By the time he became a communist he was already prominent as a leader among the railwaymen, and in 1931 he was transferred to the Transylvanian village of Dej as a disciplinary measure. From that time he added the name 'Dej' to his own rather prosaic name of Gheorghe Gheorghiu.

In 1932, he was made secretary of the railwaymen's central 'action committee' and in 1933, according to his official biography, he was responsible for leading a strike in the railway workshops at Grivita, near Bucharest. The strike was suppressed with great brutality and served to encourage the growth of fascist rule in Rumania. Gheorghiu-Dej was arrested and sentenced to twelve years' forced labour. This put an effective stop to his career as a labour leader; but he is said to have continued the work of political agitation and organisation in the prison camps. In April 1944, even before his final escape in August, he is said to have held a meeting in a prison hospital with other leaders at which the wartime leaders were removed and a new provisional secretariat was appointed, which included Emil Bodnaras. At the same time, Gheorghiu-Dej was recognised as leader of the party, apparently with the approval of the Russians and of the 'Moscow' group. Unlike many of the other people at the top of the Rumanian Communist Party, he had the great advantage of being unquestionably Rumanian and a genuine member of the working-class. It is possible that the 'Muscovites' underestimated his other qualities.

Of the other prisoners, Gheorghe Apostol's career was similar in many ways to Gheorghiu-Dej's. Born in 1912, he too was a railwayman and the son of a railwayman, had become a communist in 1930 and been arrested in 1936. Chivu Stoica, born in 1908, was also a railway worker and was also involved with Gheorghiu-Dej in the Grivita affair, for which he was sentenced to fifteen years' detention. Alexandru Moghioros, born in 1917, was of Hungarian origin, became a communist in 1930 and was arrested in 1935. Nicolae Ceausescu was born in Pitesti in 1918, joined the communists in 1932 and was leader of their youth movement by 1940.

The Moscow group was composed of people of a rather different background. Ana Pauker, one of the few women to reach the top ranks of communism, was a Jewess and the daughter of a rabbi. She had been active as a revolutionary socialist since the early 'twenties and experienced frequent imprisonment in pre-war Rumania. She was finally arrested in 1935 and sentenced to ten years in prison, from which she was released in 1940 in exchange for a Bessarabian patriot held in Russia. She then went to Moscow, where she had already spent many years before the war.

Vasile Luca was a Hungarian, born in 1898, who had been something of an international revolutionary in the 'thirties and who was liberated from prison by Russian troops when they entered the country in 1940. He spent the war years in Moscow. Emil Bodnaras was born in 1904 in the Bukovina of a Ukrainian father and a German mother. He was an officer in the Royal Rumanian Army when he deserted to Russia in 1933. He remained there until 1944, when he was sent through the fighting lines to take charge of communist activity in Rumania and establish contact with the 'native' group.

Such, briefly, were some of the people who represented Rumanian communism in Moscow and Bucharest. It would be a mistake to lay too great stress on the distinction between the 'native' and the 'Moscow' group, though they clearly saw things differently. But the mere fact of a long stay and training in Moscow did not necessarily make a man pro-Russian or tie him permanently to the Soviet 'apparatus'; any more than to spend years in a Rumanian prison necessarily made a communist less doctrinaire or more of a patriot.

In 1944 the Moscow group, led by Ana Pauker, appeared to take the view that there was no point in relying on the Rumanian Communist Party to put communism into power.

Their policy was apparently to wait for the Russian armies to over-run the country, overthrow the monarchy and the existing order and then instal a communist regime. Ana Pauker's main activity at the time was the recruitment of as many Rumanian prisoners of war as she could persuade into Rumanian units —the 'Tudor Vladimirescu' division—to fight alongside the Russians and form the backbone of an eventual Rumanian police force or even political organisation. In pursuit of this policy, the Moscow group was opposed to any collaboration with the existing regime; they saw the brightest future in the complete defeat of Rumania by the Russians.

The communist leaders in Rumania appear to have dis-approved of the idea of achieving power purely with the aid of the Soviet army. Their policy was quickly to build up an organisation within the country under communist leadership which would play a part in the overthrow of the old regime and would give the communists a legitimate voice in the country's future. They may well have been less optimistic about their chances of coming to power; but they were concerned at least to give themselves some real roots in the country.

In the event, both policies played a part in the establish-ment of communism in post-war Rumania. King Michael moved fast enough to prevent the country's being treated entirely as an enemy, so that Ana Pauker's hopes were partially dashed, though the Russian military occupation was the decisive factor in the post-war situation. But the native communists also played an important role with their organisation of the working people.

It is difficult now to determine exactly what part was played by the communists on the spot. The official account of the events of August 1944 acknowledges the importance of the arrest of Antonescu, depicting it as a major contribution to the defeat of the German armies. But it minimises the part played by King Michael and his advisers in Antonescu's removal, attributing the success of the coup primarily to the foresight of the com-munists and their activity in rallying all the sections of the population hostile to fascism and to their careful preparation of the revolt.

The communists claim that the wartime opposition among the workers, peasants and intellectuals, and even in the armed forces, was centred around their leadership. Though Gheorghiu-Dej and the other leaders were in prison, they are said to have kept in touch with the underground movement and to have worked out as early as 1943 a plan for the eventual overthrow of the dictatorship. This version of the events of August 1944 was given in 1964, on the twentieth anniversary of the coup d'état:

> The [Communist] Party realised a broad coalition of all the political groupings and circles which, for one reason or another, spoke in favour of Rumania's withdrawal from the Hitlerite war. The king and the circles around the royal palace, who saw in their participation in the removal of Antonescu their only hope of escaping serious responsibility resting with them for having dragged Rumania into the war, were obliged to accept the plan of action established by the Communist Party. This very fact meant a recognition of the decisive role played by the Communist Party of Rumania at a crucial moment in the country's destiny.

In line with this view, the communists claim that the leaders of the National Peasant and Liberal parties were obliged in June 1944 to join the National Democratic Front which the communists had formed with the Social Democratic Party in May. They claim that they had already formed fighting units and had drawn up plans for an armed insurrection with the aid of patriotic generals and other high-ranking army officers. Finally, they point to the fact that, on the night of August 9, shortly before the coup d'état, their leader, Gheorghiu-Dej, was spirited out of the Tirgu Jiu camp by Ion Gheorge Maurer, who became prime minister in 1961.

The communists do not deny the part played in the events of August 1944 by the advance of the Russian armies. This was one of the 'favourable external conditions' for Antonescu's overthrow. But the stress is now laid on other aspects: that it was a national revolt of the Rumanian people and that the driving and organising force behind it was the communists. That the communists did play an important role is suggested by the presence of Bodnaras in the palace on August 23, by the inclusion of Patrascanu, a communist, in the new government, and by the resistance to the Germans which Rumanian fighting units put up in Bucharest. But their present claim, which would imply that it was they who put the idea of arresting Antonescu into the king's head and who influenced the king's close advisers, seems to be stretching the bounds of probability too far.

On August 20, 1944, the Russians launched the offensive which was to carry them through the Balkans. The Rumanian government formally declared war on Germany on August 26. By August 30, Soviet troops had entered Bucharest and Ploesti, and by the end of September they had crossed the country, reached the Jugoslav border and swept northwards through Transylvania. In these battles the Rumanians took their duties as allies very seriously, putting 15 full divisions into the field and fighting alongside the Russian armies in pursuit of the Germans into Hungary and Czechoslovakia. Rumanian losses in this campaign were estimated at 160,000 dead.

While the Russians seem to have been glad to accept this 'brotherhood-in-arms' at this stage of the war, they behaved towards both the Rumanian military and the Rumanian civilians in the areas which they occupied as invaders and occupiers rather than as allies. Bessarabia was already irretrievably lost and in the process of being 'rerussified'. In Moldavia, the Russian forces, though meeting with no resistance from the Rumanian army, established a regime of military occupation, appointing local officials of their own choosing and cutting Moldavia off from the rest of Rumania. In Transylvania, the Dobrogea and the Banat, the Russian military and security services established complete control on the grounds that these areas were still the scene of military operations and that the war was not over. There was no one to challenge their authority.

On September 12, 1944, Britain, America and Russia concluded an armistice convention, the terms of which were largely those already demanded by the Russians, giving legal sanction to the military occupation which had already been established. In October, Winston Churchill, in Moscow for talks with Stalin about the future of Europe, proposed that the Russians should have a 'ninety per cent predominance in Rumania' in exchange for a similar 'predominance' for the Western powers in Greece: a piece of diplomatic horse-dealing to which Stalin readily agreed. From that moment the Russians were in fact the masters of Rumania, able to do with it more or less what they pleased. The Antonescu dictatorship was defeated and discredited; the organs of local and regional government had broken down; communications of all kinds were disrupted; the pre-war political parties were disorganised; and even the communists, however strong they were becoming in the capital, had no nation-wide organisation to make their influence felt. The Russian armed forces, backed by hordes of political and police 'advisers', were in 1944 and 1945 the only effective organisation in the country.

It mattered little to the Russians in 1944 that the country continued to be nominally a monarchy or that its government was by no means communist. The government formed by General Sanatescu in August 1944 was crippled in its activities because the country was still at war and effective control was in the hands of the Russian military. Nor was his second government, formed in November 1944, with the addition of Gheorghiu-Dej as minister of Transport and of Petru Groza, the amenable landowner and leader of the 'Ploughmen's Front', in a much better position to assert itself. At this stage the Russians largely ignored the civil administration, while the communists concentrated their efforts on disruptive activities in industry and among the peasants and on increasing their own prestige among the people as a whole. They aimed at achieving a degree of control over the masses which would enable them to organise 'popular' support for radical measures and protests against the palace and the democratic parties.

But by the end of 1944, when the war had passed over Rumania and life was beginning to return to normal, the Russians began to turn their attention to forcing a government on the country more adaptable to their needs. At the beginning of December street demonstrations in which there were some shooting incidents led to Sanatescu's resignation and his replacement, with Russian approval, by General Radescu, the chief of staff of the Rumanian army. His government also was a 'caretaking' coalition—with the important difference that he admitted to it a leading 'Muscovite' communist in the person of Teohari Georgescu, who became deputy minister of the Interior, under Radescu himself, thus giving the communists and their Russian advisers direct access to the country's security services.

Meanwhile the communists promoted the National Democratic Front, which had been created to provide a patriotic and popular cover for their activities and to provide a nominally non-communist organisation for all those who wanted to jump on to their political bandwagon. In January 1945, following a visit to Moscow by Gheorghiu-Dej, the Front launched a vigorous campaign for social and economic reforms, backed by demonstrations throughout Rumania. At the demonstrations in Bucharest on February 24, there were again shootings and casualties which led, as doubtless was intended, to demands for Radescu's dismissal.

Once the Yalta meeting of the Big Three was over in February, the Russians felt free to go ahead with their plans for Rumania. On February 27, Andrei Vyshinsky, the former Soviet public prosecutor turned foreign minister, arrived in Bucharest to speed up political evolution there. He demanded the removal of Radescu, on the grounds that he was incapable of maintaining order in the country, and his replacement by Petru Groza. Vyshinsky was said to have put his demands to King Michael with great violence and coarseness and to have accompanied his interview with much table-banging and door-slamming. At the same time the Russians had succeeded in getting Rumanian army units out of the capital and had arranged that Russian tanks should parade ostentatiously around the palace. Unable to obtain any effective support for his resistance to Russian pressure from the West, the young king had no choice but to yield.

The Groza government marked an important step forward for the communists. Groza himself was entirely amenable to communist direction; the members of the non-communist parties who agreed to serve represented only a section of their organisations; and the ministries of Defence, the Interior, Justice and the National Economy were all given to communists. This was sufficient for them to have a firm hold on the main branches of the administration. The government as a whole was committed to unquestioning obedience to Soviet demands.

Russian satisfaction with the new government was quickly signified in May 1945 by the demonstrative return of Transylvania to Rumanian sovereignty. This was followed in August by the Soviet government's formal recognition of the Groza government, despite opposition to this move by the Western powers. As a further demonstration of its power, the Groza government put General Antonescu on trial in May and sentenced him to death.

The pace at which things were moving prompted some reaction on the part of the king and the Allies. In August the king demanded Groza's resignation and, when the latter refused, he announced that the Crown would deny approval to the government's actions. But, confident of the backing of the Russians, Groza proceeded to ignore the king and to rule without the royal assent. When crowds gathered outside the palace on the king's birthday in November, the government did not fear to give orders to fire on them.

American and British pressure at the Moscow conference in December 1945 resulted in what appeared at first to be a partial retreat by the communists, who agreed to the admission to the government of a representative each from the National Peasant and Liberal parties and to the organisation of free elections. But the 'dilution' of the administration had no practical effect on its policies, since the non-communist members had no means of enforcing their will, whereas the Groza government received, in return for this unimportant concession, formal recognition by both the British and American governments in February 1946. It then proceeded to prepare the promised elections, which were held eventually in November. With the Russians in control of the country and the Groza government apparently approved of by the West and in a position to manipulate the electoral machinery and the press and to intimidate the political opposition, it is hardly surprising that the National Democratic Front was able to announce that it had won an overwhelming majority.

This victory for the communists was followed shortly, in February 1947, by the conclusion of the peace treaty with Rumania and by ever more confident actions on the part of the Groza government. The first half of the year was marked by a reign of terror against the democratic parties, involving large numbers of arrests, deportations and executions. July saw the arrest of the Peasant leaders, Iuliu Maniu and Ion Michalache, followed by the dissolution of both Peasant and Liberal parties in August and the trial and imprisonment of the two leaders in October. In November, there entered the government Ana Pauker, as minister for Foreign Affairs, Vasile Luca as minister of Finance and Emil Bodnaras as minister for the Armed Forces. Such a government, in which many of the key ministries were occupied by people who were not only communists, but who did not disguise their prior loyalty to Moscow and who were in some cases still Soviet citizens, could legitimately be described as a 'satellite' of Russia. It was certainly going to take no action contrary to the will of Stalin.

By this time—the end of 1947—the Russians had succeeded in imposing their will on practically every country in eastern Europe. (The exception was Czechoslovakia, which was to be brought into line early in 1948.) Bulgaria, Hungary and Poland had all been reduced to the same status of Soviet satellite and were obedient to the Russian will. The Marshall Plan for American aid in the reconstruction of Europe's damaged economies had been rejected on Stalin's orders. The 'Cominform', a sort of limited Communist International, was set up in September to bind the communist parties of eastern Europe more closely to the Soviet Union. In short, the 'iron curtain' had descended; eastern Europe was firmly under Soviet control.

In these circumstances, the continuation of Rumania as a monarchy was clearly an anachronism which had to be eradicated. King Michael had carried on bravely in the face of overwhelming Russian and communist pressure and with no effective support from the West. Now he was isolated and helpless. His abdication was finally forced by Groza and Gheorghiu-Dej with the customary threats of force and civil war. This time there was no need for Vyshinsky's stormy presence. Reluctantly and under great pressure the king signed his act of abdication. On the same day, December 30, 1947, Rumania was declared to be a 'people's republic'.

This republic was essentially a Russian creation. It was certainly not the result of a natural play of political forces within the country, though there was undoubtedly a good deal of dissatisfaction with the pre-war regimes among the people. But the one single factor which dominated all else in Rumanian political life between the middle of 1944 and the end of 1947 was the presence of Russia in the country, in the form of military units, of secret police and of 'advisers' in every ministry and institution throughout the economy. It is safe to say that during this period no decision could be taken by the Rumanian government without previous agreement with the Russians. Many of the ministers and party leaders did not wish it to be otherwise. If there were some of them, as later appeared possible, who secretly resented their dependence on the Russians, they said nothing at the time. There was, indeed, little they could say or do, for it was already clear that the fate of 'national' communists was to be as harsh as that of non-communist patriots. In 1947 the prospect of an eventual Russian retreat seemed very remote indeed, and the Rumanians—communists and non-communists alike—had to make the best of the situation and wait. Rumanians had done this before.

3

Economic Exploitation

I asked Stalin what fate he had in mind for the Balkan
States. He replied that Bulgaria, having accepted the
Allies' armistice conditions, would retain her independence, but that 'she would receive the punishment she
deserved' and that she too would have to become
'democratic'. The same would apply to Rumania.—
General de Gaulle, Mémoires de Guerre, Vol. III.

SOVIET RUSSIA was impoverished by the second world
war. By the time Russian troops stormed into Berlin and
Hitler was defeated, the Soviet Union had been bled white by
the devastation and effort of war. The western territories of the
Soviet Union had been one of the principal battle-grounds of
the war, on which the 'scorched earth' policy, first of the
Russians themselves and then of the retreating Germans, had
devastated or removed everything of value. Soviet industry had
been destroyed or transferred or turned over exclusively to
military needs. The Soviet consumer, never held in much
account, had been completely ignored for five years. Farm
production had dropped disastrously through the ravages of war
and lack of manpower. The Soviet economy was practically at
a standstill, faced with the problem of reorganisation and reconstruction, and the Soviet people were exhausted, shocked and
starving. Some twenty millions of them were dead.

The Soviet Union thus presented an unusual paradox in world history. On the one hand it was a victorious power, a member of the grand alliance with a seat at the council tables where the fate of Europe and the world was to be decided. Never before had Soviet Russia enjoyed such a status in the world. Moreover it commanded an enormous military force which now occupied the eastern half of Europe with a population of some hundred million people. On the other hand, behind this impressive and formidable front, Russia was abysmally poor and internally weak. The task of restoring Russia's economy in its basic respects to at least its pre-war level before the world became aware of Soviet weakness was Stalin's main preoccupation and the objective to which he subordinated all other interests.

To solve this problem of post-war restoration in the shortest possible time, Stalin had to make the maximum use of whatever assets he had to hand. Of these, Russia's new position as a victor nation and its domination of eastern Europe were two of the most important. His policy towards the countries of the area, including Rumania, was directed above all to extracting from them at the least cost everything that could be of value to the Soviet Union. This was the explanation of the period of intense economic exploitation to which the Soviet government subjected the countries of eastern Europe from 1944 and from which Rumania suffered worse than most.

Before the second world war Rumania was still a predominately agricultural country, with nearly eighty per cent of its twenty million population tilling the soil. The production of wheat in the pre-war decade averaged about three million tons and the production of maize about five million tons, making Rumania the biggest grain producer of all the countries of eastern Europe. Agricultural produce and timber accounted for over forty per cent of Rumania's total exports.

At the same time Rumanian industry was expanding steadily, if slowly. The net product of industry was estimated to have increased between 1925 and 1938 by about eighty per cent. The main branch was the oil industry, which produced as much as eight million tons in the years 1935-7, though this had dropped to 5.2 million tons in 1940. Steel production in 1938 stood at 277,000 tons and that of high quality coal at 290,000 tons.

Some idea of the relative state of the Rumanian economy in 1937 is provided by the figure of 295,000 million lei for the total national income. This was the equivalent at the time of $1,200 million, or roughly the same as the national income of Austria. But, whereas in the case of Austria this gave an average of between $150 and $160 per head of the population, in the case of Rumania the figure was only between $60 and $70 per head. This was slightly above the level in Bulgaria and Jugoslavia and about the same as in Greece.

In 1938, Rumania's exports, mainly oil, foodstuffs and timber, were estimated to be worth $154 m., while its imports, mainly consisting of metals, machinery, textiles and yarns, were valued at $137 m. Germany and Austria between them took 27 per cent of Rumania's exports and delivered 37 per cent of its imports. The other countries of eastern Europe accounted for less than a fifth of Rumania's foreign trade, and Russia did not feature as a trading partner at all.

The main troubles from which the pre-war Rumanian economy suffered were chronic rural overpopulation and the parcellation of farmland, coupled with lack of adequate investment both in agriculture and industry. Even in those industries, and notably the oil industry, where the rate of investment was higher, much of the capital was foreign and brought little real benefit to Rumania itself. Rumania was in fact crying out for a carefully planned agrarian reform and intensive industrialisation, which would enable the Rumanian people to reap the benefit of their country's considerable natural wealth.

Instead of this, however, the situation in Europe dictated that Rumania's agriculture and industry should become from 1940 to 1944 mere appendages of the German economy, with no benefit whatsoever to Rumania. At the same time, war wreaked its customary havoc on all aspects of Rumania's economic life, depleting the countryside and industry of manpower and disorganising the whole system. But there was even worse to come when the war ended. For then, instead of being able to devote themselves to the restoration of their own economy, the Rumanians had to stand aside and watch it being pillaged for the benefit of Russia.

Production figures for agriculture and industry in 1945 reveal what the war had done. Wheat production had fallen to 1,245,000 tons, and maize production to 1,860,000. Oil output was only 3.5 million tons in 1944, though it recovered slightly to 4.6 million tons in 1945. Steel output fell to 125,000 tons in 1945 and the output of high quality coal to 200,000 tons. Altogether the total industrial production appears to have fallen to well below half the 1938 level by the end of the war.

But, however run down it was, the Rumanian economy still represented a valuable prize to the Russians, in terms both of its real and movable assets and of current production. They used every means, from the crudest to the most refined, to transfer Rumanian wealth to Russia. It was at best a very short-sighted policy, but the Russians were the only judges at the time of the urgency of their needs. They had no time to think of the future of the countries they were exploiting.

The first and simplest method employed by the Russians to extract wealth from Rumania was straightforward pillage. This included far more than the sort of wholesale thieving of private property in which the Russian soldiery indulged in every country through which they passed as conquerors. It was not just a question of the watches and clocks that were seized by the ordinary soldiers, or of the cars and carpets that were removed by the Russian officers. The seizure of 'war booty' went much further than this, and with the obvious approval and on the instructions of the Soviet authorities. This became clear from the fact that, although Rumania broke with the Germans on August 23, 1944, and fought from that day on the Allied side, the Russians later insisted when drafting the peace treaty that Rumania had been actively engaged in fighting against the Germans only after the signing of the formal armistice on September 12. This meant that everything the Russians had seized up to that date could be regarded, and was in fact regarded by them, as legitimate 'booty'.

The booty included the whole of the Rumanian navy and the greater part of the merchant fleet, amounting to some 700 vessels. Other major items were vast quantities of equipment from the oil industry, the loss of which seriously affected oil

31

production for many years, and half the rolling stock of the Rumanian railways.

The second form of depredation of the Rumanian economy was conducted under the 'legitimate' cover of reparation payments provided for in the armistice convention. Under this heading the Rumanian government undertook to pay the Russians $300 million in the form of oil products, timber, grain and other materials. This was intended to be restitution to the Russians for losses incurred in their military operations against Rumania. In addition, Rumania was obliged to cover the costs of the Russian occupation force, to place various services at its disposal and to return everything that had been removed from Soviet territory during the war. Terms such as these imposed on a defeated nation by a desperate victor meant in fact that the Russians were able to ship back to Russia practically anything they set their eyes on: oil stocks, industrial equipment, grain, livestock. In so far as any account was made of what property was removed under the heading of reparations, it was done on the basis of 1938 world prices—a device which in some cases doubled the quantities of materials to be delivered.

A Western estimate, which has been frequently quoted, of the total value of all the goods and services taken by the Russians from September 1944 to June 1948 is $1,785 million. This would mean that Russia absorbed no less than 86 per cent of Rumania's total national income during that period.

The third method of exploitation used by the Russians was the system of joint Soviet-Rumanian companies for the management of the more important of Rumania's industries. This device was apparently designed to give the Russians control of property and equipment which they could not remove from Rumania, as well as of the output of the industries concerned. The same device was used in the Soviet Union's economic relations with certain other of its east European satellites, but nowhere with greater thoroughness or efficiency than in Rumania. The so-called 'Sovrom' companies became the symbols of Soviet economic exploitation of the satellite countries.

Joint companies were set up to handle transport, aviation, the timber industry, banking, the oil industry, the production of tractors, chemicals, gas, metals and coal, and the building industry. The arrangement in each case was that the Russians and

Rumanians should each contribute half of the share capital and have an equal share in the running of the companies and their products. In the majority of cases, however, the Russian contribution amounted to no more than the former German assets in the various industries (and sometimes assets originally belonging to France and other Allied powers) which the Soviet military had seized in 1944. Only in a few cases did the Russians send equipment from Russia to Rumania—mainly in cases where otherwise the industry would have been unable to get into production. If the Russian 'contribution' was often only nominal, however, Russian control was always complete, since the conditions of post-war occupation made nonsense of the formal 'equality' with the Rumanians. The director of most of the companies was a Russian who had the last word in the policy of the companies and in the disposition of its output.

In effect, the joint company system turned the main branches of Rumanian industry into appendages of the Soviet economy. Indeed, the Soviet-controlled enterprises enjoyed priority over those which remained under purely Rumanian control. It was significant that when, after many years of successful exploitation, Stalin died and his successors were anxious to show their willingness to relax their grip on their satellite neighbours, the joint companies were quickly dissolved. Their dissolution in 1954 was one of the first sure signs of a new Soviet policy towards eastern Europe.

Finally, among the methods of Soviet exploitation, came the trade agreement. A series of agreements was signed in the immediate post-war years, regulating the exchange of goods between Russia and Rumania and giving formal shape to the redirection of Rumanian foreign trade, which was now channelled almost exclusively to Russia and eastern Europe. While these agreements ensured that the Russians would continue to take what they needed from the Rumanian economy, they also provided for the supply to Rumania of certain materials, especially raw materials, without which Rumanian industry could not be expected to operate. As their own economy began to get on to its feet, the Russians began to realise that a policy of pure exploitation was self-defeating and that they would have to adopt a more enlightened policy if Rumanian industry was not to come to a halt. They therefore supplied substantial quantities of raw materials, such as iron and steel, coke and coal, trucks and electric motors, cotton and wool, in return for the delivery of finished manufactured goods. This seemed to be the pattern of trade which the Russians intended to maintain. The Russians also agreed in 1945 and again in 1948 to a reduction in the rate of reparations payments. They sent the Groza government loans of wheat to help overcome the serious food crises in 1945 and 1946; they returned some of Rumania's warships and cargo vessels; and they eased the conditions for the return of Soviet property. These gestures were partly intended to strengthen the hand of the pro-Russian regime which had by then been installed. But they were also a confirmation of the extortionate demands that had been imposed on the Rumanian economy. Even at their reduced level they left Rumania tied hand and foot to Soviet Russia.

In view of the political and social upheavals that were taking place in the country, it was not surprising that the Rumanian economy was slow to recover after the war. Not until about 1950 was it restored to approximately its pre-war level. Oil production did not rise above five million tons until 1950; coal output exceeded the pre-war peak level for the first time in 1949; the output of ferrous metals just exceeded the 1938 level in 1948; the production of cotton and woollen textiles was still at about the 1938 level in 1949. In agriculture the progress was even slower, the production of wheat and maize in 1951 being still below the pre-war level, though the number of livestock had been more or less restored in 1948.

But this restoration of economic activity and increase in the production of goods brought no benefit whatsoever to the Rumanian people, since the better part of what they were producing was being syphoned off and sent to Russia. Indeed, by 1947 the country was in the throes of a grave economic crisis, marked by widespread hunger, empty shops and runaway inflation.

In 1948, however, following the abdication of the king and the installation of a predominantly communist regime, the Russians, doubtless under pressure from the Rumanian communists, realised that there was a limit to the extent to which they could exploit the Rumanian economy without giving anything in return. In June 1948 Stalin agreed to the reduction of outstanding reparations payments by half. In December the minister for Foreign Trade, Alexandru Barladeanu, went to Moscow and negotiated agreements providing for a substantial increase in trade between Russia and Rumania and for Soviet technical aid to the Rumanian economy. The Russians undertook to supply substantial quantities of industrial equipment, motor vehicles, agricultural machinery and various raw materials.

At the same time, the Rumanian communists began to introduce into the economy a system of overall planning on the Soviet pattern. After having carried through two 'one-year' plans for 1949 and 1950, they drew up a five-year plan to cover the years 1951-5, setting highly ambitious production targets for the main branches of industry. The plan placed great stress on the expansion of heavy industry and of Rumania's industrial potential in general, and was very similar in general structure to the plans in force in the Soviet Union and the other communist countries. This was due at any rate in part to the fact that it had been drawn up with the help of Russian planners and of economists from the communist countries of eastern Europe.

It was at this time that the Russians began to take the first steps towards co-ordinating all the economies of eastern Europe with their own. In June 1947 General George Marshall, then United States secretary of state, had outlined a plan designed 'to place Europe on its feet economically'. His offer of substantial American aid for a European plan of economic reconstruction was extended to all the countries of Europe, including those in the Soviet sphere of influence. The immediate reaction of some of the communist governments which had by then been installed in power, and notably those of the Czechs and Poles, had been to welcome the offer. But Stalin, ever conscious of the relative weakness of the Soviet economy compared with America's and only too aware of his own inability to compete with the Americans in economic patronage, forced the satellite governments to reject the 'Marshall Plan'.

The acceptance of this plan by the countries of western Europe, however, and the progress which they began to make towards economic recovery forced Stalin to take some comparable action in the East. This took the form of the creation in

January 1949 of the Council for Mutual Economic Assistance, which came later to be known in the West as 'Comecon'. The original members of the organisation were: the Soviet Union, Poland, Czechoslovakia, Hungary, Bulgaria and Rumania. These were later joined by Albania and East Germany as full members. Much later, in 1956, after Marshal Tito's reconciliation with the Russian leaders, Jugoslavia began to attend meetings as an observer. Communist China, Outer Mongolia, North Korea and North Vietnam have also participated in the Council's work as observers at various times. But it has functioned primarily as an organisation linking the countries of eastern Europe with the Soviet Union. Since it was mainly within this organisation that Rumania's resistance to Russian domination was conducted, it will be necessary to enter in some detail into its history and policies.

The declared purpose of the Council for Mutual Economic Assistance was 'to develop economic collaboration between the socialist countries and to co-ordinate their economic progress on the basis of the equality of rights of all the member states, by organising the exchange of economic and technical experience and by extending aid to each other in the form of raw materials, foodstuffs and equipment'. There was in fact no suggestion that the countries of eastern Europe were going to be the recipients of the kind of massive aid that America was beginning to pour into western Europe, even if they might hope to benefit from guaranteed supplies from Russia. Indeed, in its early stages Comecon was little more than a body through which the Russians could supervise the foreign trade of the satellite states and ensure that they themselves derived the maximum benefit from the satellite economies and that the western powers were excluded from east European markets. As the principal Polish newspaper said later: 'In the initial phase of its existence Comecon limited its activities to the field of commercial relations and took only a marginal interest in problems of production.' In any case, the Russians had no need of such an economic organisation to assure their grip on eastern Europe, which depended much more on the physical presence in the countries themselves of Russian military and police officers and of Russian advisers throughout the economy and administration. The time had not yet come when they would have to resort to economic weapons to retain their hold. Comecon remained a relatively ineffective organisation until Stalin's death in 1953.

The first major change in relations between Russia and the countries of eastern Europe came after Stalin died. In their anxiety to soften the impact of their rule and avert revolt, the Russians brought reparations to an end, dissolved the iniquitous 'joint companies' and began to trade with eastern Europe on rather fairer terms at prices more closely related to those prevailing in world markets at the time.

But at the same time the first moves were made, as though to compensate for the rather looser political relationship, to turn Comecon into an instrument for planning and directing the economic activity of the Soviet bloc as a whole. From 1954 to 1956 there was much talk of the need for the 'socialist camp' to become economically self-sufficient, to avoid the duplication of productive efforts and to co-ordinate the economic plans of the various countries. The meeting of the Council held in East Berlin in May 1956 saw the first serious attempt to co-ordinate the economic development of the bloc on a long-term basis. But at that time it was not so much a question of genuine collaboration between all the member countries as of the Russians telling the other countries what they should and should not do. There was no suggestion that priorities and productive capacities in the Soviet Union should be dictated by the Comecon countries as a whole.

Whatever plans the Russians may have had for Comecon at the time were completely upset by political developments at the end of 1956. The revolt of the Hungarian people, the near-revolt in Poland and the spirit of unrest that spread throughout eastern Europe forced the Russians first to take emergency measures that had nothing to do with the plans of Comecon and then to seek to devise more flexible policies towards eastern Europe as a whole.

Even before the Hungarian uprising had been finally suppressed the Soviet government had issued, on October 30, a declaration on its relations with the other communist states. In what was one of the frankest statements the Russians had ever made about their relations with their neighbours, they admitted 'many difficulties, unresolved problems and downright mistakes, including mistakes in mutual relations among the socialist countries—violations and errors which demeaned the principle of equality in relations among the socialist states'. The Declaration said that the Soviet government had already criticised these mistakes, but 'recent events' made it necessary for them to make a formal declaration on their relations with eastern Europe 'particularly in the economic and military spheres'. They were now prepared, the Declaration said, to revise their economic relations with the governments of eastern Europe with full recognition of national sovereignty; they were ready to consider the withdrawal from eastern Europe of the Russian specialists—'engineers, agronomists, scientists, military advisers'—whom they had sent there after the war; and they were prepared to discuss with the governments of Hungary, Rumania and East Germany the question of the Soviet troops still stationed in those countries.

This Declaration attracted relatively little attention in the world at the time, and with good reason, since Soviet troops were still busy terrorising the Hungarian population and the prospect of their withdrawing from there or from the other countries seemed very remote. Nevertheless it was a very important and unusual admission by the Russians that they had been exploiting eastern Europe economically and dominating the countries by means of their numerous personnel and troops.

However meaningless it might sound in October 1956, their promise to reform was one which the Rumanians at any rate took seriously. *Scanteia,* the official newspaper of the Rumanian communists, on November 2, 1956, hailed the Declaration as 'a veritable code of correct relations between free peoples'. The principles it enunciated were in fact to serve the Rumanians as a platform in their resistance to the Russians.

At the end of November, Chivu Stoica, the prime minister, led an economic delegation to Moscow for talks, which resulted in a Russian promise to deliver considerably increased quantities of raw materials, industrial plant and wheat. It is also possible that, taking the Russians at their word, the prime minister had at least some preliminary talks with the Russians about the removal of their troops. The Russians were at this time in a chastened and amenable mood, willing to extend large credits in the hope of keeping the tide of revolt from spreading in eastern Europe. They were still in this openhanded mood when Comecon held its Eighth Council meeting in Warsaw in June 1957.

The Rumanians were also quick to revise their own economic plans in the light of the Russians' new attitude. At the end of December 1956 they cut capital investment for 1957 by 15 per cent. The rate planned for the increase in industrial production was reduced from 13.6 per cent in 1956 to only 5.4 per cent in 1957. This meant the abandonment of some of Rumania's more ambitious industrial projects. At the same time, industrial workers were granted a substantial increase in wages and bonus payments, while the Rumanian farmer was relieved of the burden of compulsory deliveries to the state from the beginning of 1957. In this way the Rumanian government took some of the tension out of its relations with the population and ensured that no Hungarian situation was likely to develop in Rumania.

But the Russians' admission of their mishandling of relations with their allies and the steps they took to appease them did not mean that they were happy to see the countries of eastern Europe go their own way or that they had modified in any way their general objective of subordinating eastern Europe to their wishes. It meant rather that they had to seek less crude and less clumsy methods by which to bind eastern Europe to the Soviet chariot. And this is what they set out to do, through the medium of Comecon, in 1957 and 1958.

The Comecon session which took place in Warsaw in June 1957 marked a further step forward in the introduction of co-ordinated long-term planning for all the member countries. The Russians had been forced to abandon their own Sixth Five-Year Plan for the years 1956 to 1960 and had announced that it would be replaced by a Seven-Year Plan to cover the years 1959 to 1965. The other countries were invited to draw up similar plans to coincide with the Soviet plan and also to look further ahead with plans covering periods of ten to fifteen years. At the same time, a good deal of work was done by the permanent commissions in the Council on problems of integration, specialisation and standardisation.

In May 1958, the leaders of all the communist parties of the countries of Comecon were summoned to Moscow for a 'summit' meeting at which the measures that had been elaborated during the previous year were put together in the form of a general directive for the future work of the organisation. The party leaders appear to have accepted the need for the closer co-ordination of their national economic plans on a long-term basis and to have agreed to the principle of the 'socialist division of labour on an international scale'. This latter doctrine, which was to mean in practice the acceptance by each country of a certain limited economic function in the communist world, was later to be a major bone of contention between the Rumanians and the Russians.

The debates in the Comecon organisation are not held in public, so that it is not known whether in the summer of 1958 differences of opinion were already being expressed. In view of later developments it seems probable that they were. The Russians had clearly decided that, if they could no longer hope to hold their newly acquired east European empire together purely by direct political or military means, there was still no reason why they should not achieve the same ends by making the communist countries economically dependent upon Russia and upon each other. Their economies could become so deeply involved in each other and their long-term plans so interwoven that it would become impossible for them to detach themselves from the 'camp'. Economics were, after all, at the root of everything, in the marxist view, and they might well provide the surest means of ensuring political stability in eastern Europe. It was this subtler approach to the problems of empire that the Russians began to put into effect in 1957 and 1958.

Unfortunately for their plans, their potential victims were also marxists who had been taught the importance of the economic factor in a nation's life. They can hardly have been reassured by the Russians' stress on long-term planning and commitments. But in the summer of 1958 none of the eastern European leaders appears to have dared or cared to oppose the Russian plans, which in any case then amounted to no more than directives for the future. Sufficient agreement was reached at the Moscow 'summit' meeting for the ninth Council meeting, held in Bucharest in June 1958, to approve the new policy of long-term co-ordination and the international division of labour. A permanent commission was set up to deal with this latter problem.

40

The elements of the forthcoming conflict were already present in the decisions of mid-1958. But there were good reasons why the conflict should not break out into the open at that point. The Russians, for their part, were still treading warily in eastern Europe, with the memory of Hungary still fresh in their minds. At the same time as they introduced their long-term plans they continued to accept the principle of equality between Comecon members and to extend aid to the less fortunate ones. Meanwhile the member countries were still too weak economically to stand up to the Russians. They were presumably still waiting to see how much benefit they would gain from the Russians' post-Hungarian mood, and, in any case, they had few contacts with the non-communist world.

There was an even more cogent reason for discretion on the part of those leaders in eastern Europe who might feel inclined to oppose the Russians. However repentant the Russians appeared after the Hungarian revolt, the fact remained that they had shown their teeth on that occasion and that their troops still bestrode both Hungary and Rumania. It would obviously have been unwise for anyone, and the Rumanians in particular, to do anything that might persuade the Russians to delay their departure. Better get the Russian troops out of the country first!

This is exactly what the Rumanians proceeded to do. In April 1957 they had concluded an agreement with the Russians regularising the terms on which Soviet units were to remain in Rumania. A year later, in May 1958, at the same time as the 'summit' meeting of east European leaders was being held in Moscow, a meeting of the Warsaw Pact announced that Soviet troops were shortly to be withdrawn from Rumania. The withdrawal began apparently at the beginning of July, and on July 25 the Rumanians announced that all Soviet forces had departed. This was a remarkable achievement for the Rumanian leaders which presumably marked the beginning of a period of far greater autonomy in the conduct of their domestic affairs and appeared to reflect the Kremlin's complete confidence in the stability of Gheorghiu-Dej's regime and in its loyalty to Moscow. The terms on which the Rumanians secured the withdrawal of the Russian presence in their country have never been revealed.

41

But it may be assumed that, until the troops were gone, the Rumanian leaders did not reveal the nature of their further ambitions.

There were in 1957 two other important developments in the communist world which were ultimately to play an important part in the Rumanian leaders' relations with Russia. November 1957 saw the fortieth anniversary of the Russian Revolution and the gathering in Moscow of communist leaders from every part of the world. It was not, however, purely an occasion for celebration. Important and often heated discussions took place behind the scenes about the world strategy of communism, and it was in the course of these debates that the existence of major differences of opinion between the Russians under Khrushchev's 'revisionist' rule and the Chinese communists, led by Mao Tse-tung, became apparent. The leaders of the twelve communist parties then in power issued at the end of their meeting a Declaration on the general line of their policy which was wordy and imprecise but which appeared to reflect the basic unity of which the communist world boasted. But those, like the Rumanian leaders, who took part in the drafting of this document must already have been aware of the gathering tension between the two major communist powers. It cannot have failed to occur to the Rumanians, and possibly to other communist leaders also, that such a division of authority in the communist world could be exploited to their own advantage.

However 'dogmatic' their views, the Chinese were, within the context of the dispute in the communist movement, the defenders of national independence in the face of Russian attempts to dictate policy. They could thus become the allies of any communist leaders who sought to throw off Russian control. They were bound to welcome the inclusion in the Moscow Declaration, probably at Chinese instigation, of a passage such as the following:

> Socialist countries base their relations on the principles of complete equality, respect for territorial integrity, state independence and sovereignty, and non-interference in one another's affairs. These are vital principles. But they do not exhaust the essence of relations between them. Fraternal mutual aid is part and parcel of these relations.... The socialist states also advocate the general expansion of economic and cultural rela-

tions with all other countries, provided they desire it, on the basis of equality, mutual benefit and non-interference in internal affairs.

This formula could reasonably be interpreted by the rulers of communist states, especially the smaller and less advanced ones —and it was so interpreted at least by the Rumanian leaders— to mean that they had the right to complete autonomy in the conduct of their own affairs, that they were entitled to expect 'fraternal' aid from Russia and other communist states, and that they were also free to develop their relations with the non-communist world. Such a formula left those who subscribed to it free to pursue practically any economic policy they pleased. For those rulers in eastern Europe who were seeking greater economic freedom, it was comforting to know that they had the backing of the Chinese against the Russians.

It may not have been entirely fortuitous, therefore, that shortly after the Moscow meeting the Rumanian prime minister, Chivu Stoica, went out of his way to tell an American newspaper correspondent that his government was ready to spend over $100,000,000 on industrial equipment in the United States, or —if American policy did not permit it—in western Europe. He announced that Rumania had a favourable balance of payments and was able to pay in dollars for equipment from American and west European manufacturers. This was the first official indication of the direction in which the Rumanian leaders were moving.

One other development in the communist world which was to affect Rumania's capacity to bargain took place in 1957 and the beginning of 1958. This was the year of Nikita Khrushchev's final victory over the 'anti-party group' in his own party. In July 1957, he ousted Molotov, Malenkov and his other opponents from the leadership of the Soviet communist party, and in March 1958 he became prime minister as well as first secretary of the party. Whatever the exact nature of the differences between him and his opponents was, it is probably safe to say that Molotov stood for a policy of stricter control of the satellites from Moscow, while Khrushchev, though not wishing to dismantle the east European empire, was less sure in his handling of its problems. His assumption of power in Moscow may well have been welcomed in Bucharest, even though the Rumanian leaders were later to fall out with him.

There was one final factor that provided the Rumanians with the indispensable base for any show of independence vis-à-vis Moscow: the Rumanian economy was beginning to show the results of ten years' concentration on intensive industrialisation. By 1958, Rumania's gross industrial output, according to official statistics, was nearly four times greater than it had been in 1938 and four and a half times greater than in 1948. It had more than doubled since 1955. Compared with 1938, the gross output of coal was over two and a half times as great, that of petroleum more than twice, that of ferrous metallurgy over five times, and that of engineering and metal working industries well over eight times as great. Rumania was well on the way to becoming an industrial nation with a more evenly balanced economy. When it is borne in mind that among the products of Rumanian industry (though the quantities are unknown) are both gold and uranium, Stoica's claim that Rumania could pay for imports from the West in dollars may not have been an empty boast.

Thus, by the middle of 1958, Rumania's position in relation to Russia had changed considerably. The Rumanian leaders were firmly in the saddle, the Rumanian economy was making it possible for the country to stand on its own feet, and the hosts of Russian troops, advisers and controllers had departed. The ultimate effect of the Hungarian revolt seemed to have been to put the Russians on the defensive, while Khrushchev's ascendancy in Moscow promised a softer Russian grip on eastern Europe. There were many reasons why the Rumanians should feel that the time had come for them to press their case more forcefully.

4

Communism and Communists

The Rumanian Workers' Party is the organised vanguard detachment of the working class, the leading
force of the people in the Rumanian People's Republic. The Party's leading role in the country's
political and state life is recorded in the Constitution.
—*Rumania in Brief, Bucharest, 1962.*

COMMUNISM was not a major force in pre-war Rumania.
Under the influence of events in Russia and the promptings
of the Communist International, in 1921, a communist movement was founded, as in many other countries, by a break-away
from the Social Democratic Party. It was a largely clandestine
organisation, soon to be forced into illegality by the authorities.
It commanded little following among the industrial workers,
and it was torn with conflict between various groups of
'Bessarabians', 'Rumanians', 'workers' and 'intellectuals'. It
was also subject to continual harassment and penetration by
the police.

Scope for the type of activity on which communists base
their movement was in any case severely limited in Rumania in
the inter-war years. Even by 1940 there were only 800,000
industrial workers in the country, and the Social Democratic
party, which enjoyed a legal existence, could not count on a

following of more than 50,000 workers. Nevertheless, in the elections of 1927 and 1931 the communists, campaigning as the United Workers' and Peasants' Bloc, won about 75,000 votes, and in 1931 gained five seats in the parliament.

Communist-led activities in industry spread to such an extent by 1933, feeding on the economic crisis which affected the whole world, that the authorities clamped down on them, with the result that the Bloc obtained only 3,500 votes in the 1933 election. The social democrats and the trade unionists refused to form a united organisation with the communists, and in 1936 the authorities succeeded in rounding up practically all the leaders of Rumanian communism and putting them in gaol. At the outbreak of the second world war there was virtually no communist party in Rumania.

During the war against Russia, the Antonescu regime was able to continue its suppression of all communist activity. But when the tide of war turned and the Rumanian workers saw the prospect of a Russian victory, there was a flood of new members into the Social Democratic Party, which emerged from the war as by far the most influential organisation among the working people. When in August 1944 the Antonescu regime was overthrown, although the communists were able to resume their activities in the light of day, they were said to have no more than a thousand members in their ranks.

A year and a half later, however, at the end of 1945, the Rumanian Communist Party claimed a membership of half a million. Despite many subsequent additions to the ranks and purges from them, it is probably fair to say that a large proportion of that initial half million still form the backbone of the party, which has a membership today of over 800,000. Where did they come from?

One source was certainly the Rumanian working-class. Not only those who had looked to the communists for leadership in the pre-war years but also many others who were dissatisfied with their lot and, encouraged by the presence of Russian troops, threw in their lot with the communists. But far more turned to the social democrats.

A more important source of members was the 'Tudor Vladimirescu' division which had been recruited in Russia from among Rumanian forces who had been defeated there or who had lain down their arms. Some of the officers and men refused to follow the new direction of their government and to fight side by side with the Russian forces they had been fighting against. But many, reluctant to rot in a Russian prison camp and naturally anxious to be on the winning side, responded to the appeals aimed at them by the Rumanian communists who had accompanied the Russian forces into Rumania. Prominent among these latter was Ana Pauker, who was eager to see the Russian troops over-run Rumania as quickly as possible. Some of the officers and men who had been prisoners in Russia had been subjected to a measure of indoctrination and could claim to know what communism was. But the majority of them had little interest in political ideas.

Ideology was not in any case an obstacle to membership at the time of Ana Pauker's recruitment campaign. According to Gheorghiu-Dej (who in 1961 described this period of Ana Pauker's activities), she had, in November 1944, told the members of the fascist Iron Guard organisation that the communists would 'gladly receive them and shake hands with them', and she had concluded an agreement with the leaders of the Iron Guard for the absorption of their membership into the Rumanian Communist Party. Ana Pauker's actions in this connection, Gheorghiu-Dej said, 'led to a relaxation of vigilance and thus permitted many members of the Iron Guard and of other fascist organisations to penetrate the party and made it possible for hostile elements to become members of the party, to organise anarchist activities and to violate the policy of the party and the laws of the country'. Later, he said, when steps were taken to check the origins of the party membership, 'hundreds of thousands of opportunists, careerists and other hostile Iron Guard elements were expelled from the party'.

Apart from these two important fields for recruitment, the party certainly acquired a large number of new supporters from among the middle-class, the provincial and local government officials and members of the civil service whose services were needed by the new regime and who were eager enough to secure their jobs by jumping on the communist bandwagon.

What the vast majority of these new recruits had in common was that they did not join the Communist Party because they were convinced communists, or even because they were convinced of the rightness of communist policy. Nor were they necessarily believers in radical social and economic reform. Least of all were they necessarily pro-Russian in their sentiments. They were thinking primarily of their own security and they joined the party which seemed most likely to ensure it.

It seems likely that the majority of those Rumanians who shared socialist ideas of some kind found their way in 1944 and 1945 into the ranks of the Social Democratic Party. That party certainly enjoyed a considerable influx of members, although even by 1948 it could claim a total of only about 200,000. In that year, the Social Democratic Party was merged with the Communist Party to form the Rumanian Workers' Party as the resultant organisation was, and still is, called. This produced a total membership in 1950 of 720,000, which was reduced through a process of purging to 580,000 in 1956. The membership today is 1,240,000. This number doubtless includes communists of all sorts: some who joined during the period of indiscriminate recruitment at the end of the war; some who had been communists even before the war; some who joined for purely personal reasons but who have subsequently convinced themselves of the rightness of communism; and some young people who have grown up under the communist regime and for whom the Communist Party represents the 'establishment' which offers the only road to power or success. But only a handful of the members are people who became communists to fight for the ideas of communism in the difficult times. The overwhelming majority of them entered the party when it was already the source of power and advancement. Membership did not mean persecution and prison, but a safe job, even if it might involve risks and responsibilities. This party is the instrument with which the leaders of Rumanian communism have to rule their country; it is the instrument which has to be kept sharp and its components content if their rule is to be unshaken; the nature of this instrument determines to a certain extent what the leaders can and cannot do.

Who are the leaders? In a dictatorial state, ruled by a party which is strictly disciplined and semi-military in organisation, the character and outlook of the men at the top are of great importance. This is particularly true in the case of Rumania.

The leaders of communist Rumania today are the men who compose the Politburo and Secretariat of the Central Committee of the Rumanian Communist (Workers') Party. These are the men who make policy and supervise its execution. There are nine full members of the Politburo and five 'candidate' members. Three of them, with the addition of one man not in the Politburo, compose the Secretariat. These fifteen men are the rulers of Rumania today.

The members of the Politburo at the time of writing are: Gheorghe Gheorghiu-Dej, Chivu Stoica, Gheorghe Apostol, Emil Bodnaras, Petre Borila, Nicolae Ceausescu, Alexandru Draghici, Alexandru Moghioros and Ion Gheorghe Maurer. The candidate members are: Dumitriu Coliu, Leonte Rautu, Leontin Salajan, Stefan Voitec and Alexandru Barladeanu. The Secretariat is composed of: Gheorghiu-Dej, Ceausescu, Stoica and Mihai Dalea.

There are a number of important features which the majority of these men have in common. In the first place, the great majority of them are apparently Rumanians by birth. Only a handful of them are non-Rumanians: Moghioros and Salajan being Hungarian by birth, Rautu being a Jew from Bessarabia. Bodnaras is of mixed Ukrainian and German origin. Maurer's father was apparently a member of the German minority in Transylvania.

Even more important, the great majority of them were active as communists in Rumania in the inter-war years. However limited their activity was, it was carried on among Rumanian workers and intellectuals. They were not 'international' communists. Five of the nine Politburo members, including Gheorghiu-Dej himself, were arrested in the mid-thirties and remained in Rumanian prisons until 1944. Only a few of them—Bodnaras, Borila, Coliu, Rautu—spent the war years in Russia and were exposed to all the pressure and indoctrination which that involved.

Most of the present circle of leaders have now known each other and worked together for nearly thirty years. Many of them are bound to each other by acts of personal friendship or courage. Thus Maurer, who was a lawyer before the war, defended many communists in the courts and later used his position to establish liaison between Gheorghiu-Dej in prison and the party outside, and it was he who organised Gheorghiu-Dej's escape from prison in August 1944. Finally, they are a relatively young group of men, of whom the eldest, Bodnaras, is only sixty, and the youngest, Draghici, is only forty-seven. On the surface at least, they would seem to make a good team.

The leaders of Rumanian communism were not always so united. The present unity, which has lasted fairly consistently since 1957, was forged in the course of very bitter political battles in the post-war period. As we have seen, the new leadership at the end of the war was formed out of two distinct elements: the 'Moscow' group led by Ana Pauker, and the 'native' group led by Gheorghiu-Dej. The latter group were not content to await the arrival of their comrades from Moscow before they set about the task of reactivating the party, and they were greatly helped in this work by Bodnaras, whose job it was to build up an organisation on the spot. But once the 'Muscovites' had returned to Bucharest, they inevitably dominated the party organisation because they enjoyed the support and confidence of the Russians, who were supreme. This dominance was reflected in the composition of the first post-war Politburo appointed by the party's national conference in October 1944. It consisted of Gheorghiu-Dej, Pauker, Luca, Georgescu, Stoica, Vasilichi and Constantinescu. Gheorghiu-Dej was made secretary-general, but the three leading 'Muscovites'—Pauker, Luca and Georgescu—were also made secretaries and were apparently able to dictate policy.

Many years later, in 1961, Gheorghiu-Dej described the situation which existed in the leadership of the party immediately after the war. Pauker and her friends, he said, acted quite independently of the Central Committee and of the Politburo. 'All important party problems were now solved by the Secretariat, where they had a majority and where on many important problems the secretary-general was in a minority.' He said that the Pauker group had used 'methods of terror and intimidation', and that there was 'no comrade in today's party leadership whose dignity as a communist and as a human being they did not offend'. At one point Pauker had started to hint that the time had come for a 'purge' among the top leaders of the party and gave instructions to the secret police to 'watch top officials of the party and government and to tap their telephone conversations, not excepting even the secretary-general of the party himself'. Ghcorghiu-Dej said that throughout the period from September 1944 until May 1952, when the Pauker group was finally expelled from the leadership, 'there was no question of a collective leadership in the Central Committee, Politburo or Secretariat'. In other words, the secretary-general was claiming that he and his supporters were helpless and therefore not responsible for the policies pursued at the time. This may well have been true. In the conditions existing in eastern Europe while Stalin was alive, serious opposition to his policies met with severe reprisals. But it must be said that, if Gheorghui-Dej and the 'native' communists were in disagreement with the Pauker group, they gave no evidence of such opposition whatsoever and were as dutifully 'stalinist' as anyone else in their public pronouncements.

In view of the apparently impregnable position the Pauker group occupied, it was all the more remarkable that Gheorghiu-Dej succeeded in removing them from power even before Stalin, who had appeared to be their main support, died in March 1953. A full year before this the Central Committee recorded disapproval of the activities of Pauker, Luca and Georgescu; and, despite their efforts to fight back, they were all three expelled from the leadership of the party in May. From this time there appears never to have been any serious challenge to Gheorghiu-Dej's leadership of the party.

His defeat of Pauker appears to have been a long, carefully planned operation. Perhaps the decisive factor in it was the wave of anti-semitism which swept across the Soviet Union and eastern Europe in the later years of Stalin's life and which found its most notable expression in the trial and execution of the Czech communist leader, Rudolf Slansky, at the end of 1952. The underlying motives for this gruesome period of crude racialism are still not clear. But there is no doubt that Stalin and his henchmen were so carried away by this campaign that they were ready to sacrifice their most devoted lieutenants in eastern Europe (of whom Slansky was certainly one) if they were Jewish. The fact that Ana Pauker was a Jewess was a powerful weapon in Gheorghiu-Dej's hands in what was at that time his competition for Stalin's favour or at least approval. But it must be said that he did not himself exploit racial prejudices within the Rumanian party in his battle with Pauker; nor did he follow the example of the Czech communists in their treatment of Slansky and have Pauker executed, though this was certainly within his power in 1952. (She continued to live in Bucharest under some form of restraint until 1960, when she died of cancer.)

The simple fact that Gheorghiu-Dej had a weapon with which he could discredit Pauker in Stalin's eyes is not, however, sufficient to explain how he was able to find an opportunity to use it. According to one account, Gheorghiu-Dej himself was under house arrest during the later period of Pauker's ascendancy, and it is said that he had to escape from his captors and fly to Moscow by special plane to argue his case with Stalin. He must have found some way of by-passing the Muscovites and their Russian collaborators in Rumania in order to gain Stalin's confidence.

It is possible, however, that Gheorghiu-Dej's victory was founded primarily on the work which he and his supporters had done inside the Rumanian Communist Party over a long period. Even as early as 1948 the party membership had been subjected to its first 'verification' campaign : a process of careful combing out of the personnel and checking of members' qualifications, both political and professional. This first campaign lasted until May 1950 and resulted in the expulsion from the party of about 192,000 members. This was followed in March 1951 by the election of new officials throughout the party organisation. The result appears to have been to reduce drastically the influence of the Pauker group within the party and to increase the influence of the younger generation of technicians upon whom Gheorghiu-Dej was to rely increasingly. This stress on the recruitment of people with good technical and professional qualifications was of great importance for the later development of policy, because it meant that the Rumanian Communist Party was much more closely in touch with the development of industry and its problems than were many other east European parties. As Ghita Ionescu says in his study of Rumanian communism :* 'The party had become from the beginning mainly a machine for supervising difficult economic and administrative work'. A similar tendency was still apparent in 1958, when Gheorghiu-Dej spoke about the party's duties in the economic field :

* *Communism in Rumania, 1944-1962* (London and New York, Oxford University Press, 1964).

To be able to work with full competence in this field, to exert a more qualified party control on the activities of the administrative managements of the enterprises, and concentrate the efforts on the more important problems, it is necessary that the party organs and organisations study and better understand the technical and economic problems, and the problems of organisation and planning of the enterprise. They must analyse in a more systematic manner the various aspects of the production process, must know well the local possibilities, and must mobilise the workers, engineers and technicians, and administrative cadres for the elemination of shortcomings and for the achievement of good results in the fulfilment of the plan tasks in all indices.

More attention must be paid to strengthening the economic commissions attached to the regional party committees and they must be provided with well-qualified cadres. Leading workers, engineers, technicians, and economists with wide experience must be attracted to the party *aktiv,* so that the party committees can base themselves on these people in the solution of economic problems.

At all events, the defeat of Ana Pauker was undoubtedly a turning-point in the post-war history of the Rumanian communist regime and an event of critical importance for the future direction of Rumanian policy. Whatever Gheorghiu-Dej and his followers stood for—and this was not yet clear—Pauker and her group certainly represented the crudest kind of subservience to Moscow, though they could not be accused of that at the time. They had also been responsible for the recruitment into the party of all sorts of opportunist and careerist elements without much consideration for political beliefs. Their removal was an essential preliminary in the process of reducing direct Russian influence over Rumania: a process which was naturally to gather pace after Stalin's death in 1953.

There was, however, another episode which was less to the credit of Gheorghiu-Dej and his supporters. This was the trial in April 1954 and the condemnation to death of Lucretiu Patrascanu, the leader who had generally been regarded as the most 'national' in his approach to communism. He had carried on political activity in Rumania throughout the war and was recognised as one of the party's leaders even before Gheorghiu-Dej was released from gaol. He was the communist admitted to the first Sanatescu government after August 23, 1944, and he also led the Rumanian delegation at the armistice talks with the Russians in 1944. But he was not appointed to the top leadership of the party in the post-war period, apparently because of differences with both of the rival contenders for power at the time.

Patrascanu was an obvious target for the Moscow-orientated leaders in 1948, when 'national' communists were being singled out for attack throughout eastern Europe and when Stalin was already preparing for his conflict with Marshal Tito. At the congress of the Rumanian Communist Party in February 1948, Patrascanu was duly attacked for his various 'deviations', which seemed to have little to do with his actual political beliefs and activities, and expelled from the Central Committee. From that point he ceased to hold any public position and was probably in prison.

It would, however, have been reasonable to expect that, after Pauker's defeat and Stalin's death, Patrascanu would be released and that some of the charges against him would be withdrawn, even if he were not elevated to the top leadership of the party. But this did not happen. Instead he was tried in April 1954, along with an oddly assorted group of people who had fallen out of favour, including Koffler, who with Foris had led the wartime activities of the party. Both Patrascanu and Koffler were sentenced to death and executed.

The trial was held behind closed doors. But, according to an account by a Rumanian who claims to have been present, Patrascanu defended himself vigorously and bravely against the charges and challenged some of the prosecution witnesses to such good effect that they were withdrawn from the case. He is said to have defended himself as a communist and to have re-affirmed his communist faith while rejecting the distortions of communism as practised in Rumania.

It is difficult to believe that Patrascanu represented a real threat to Gheorghiu-Dej in 1954; he might well have been a political asset to him. Nevertheless the Rumanians permitted Patrascanu to be judicially murdered. This remains one of the more obscure episodes in the history of Rumanian communism and one which it is difficult to excuse even in a country where politics has always been a game played rather roughly. The official explanation remains that he was in fact the agent of a Western power.

The Politburo and Secretariat appointed in May 1952 contained a clear majority of the 'native' communists. Gheorghiu-Dej was supreme, and he signalled the victory by having himself made prime minister as well as secretary of the party. There was one further 'purge' of the leadership, however, in June 1957, just before Khrushchev succeeded in defeating the Molotov-Malenkov opposition in the leadership of the Soviet Communist Party. The Rumanian purge brought about the downfall of Chisinevschi and Constantinescu, both until then members of the Politburo and both in their different ways very able men. Later accounts of their downfall indicated that they had both challenged Gheorghiu-Dej's leadership of the party in 1956 and that they had been removed primarily because they, or at least Constantinescu, was a rival for Gheorghiu-Dej's position. Constantin Parvulescu, the veteran leader who was also prominent during the war years, was ousted in 1961 for alleged complicity with Constantinescu and Chisinevschi. But none of the three apparently suffered the fate of Patrascanu.

Since 1957, therefore, the leadership of the Rumanian Communist Party has been very stable, and the nine members of the present Politburo have been members of that body since 1952. They are a homogeneous group, all the members of which have everything to gain from keeping the present regime in power in Rumania and from making it a successful regime in the eyes of at least a substantial and influential section of the population. They appear to agree that this means above all making Rumania *economically* successful and that in the modern world success is not measured so much in terms of military prowess or of political ideas as of standards of living. The Rumanian leaders appear to realise that, unless they can fulfil some of the claims to economic progress and social advancement that communism makes, their own justification for remaining in control of affairs will be lost.

5

The Basis of Independence

'Rapid and all-round industrialisation.'

THE revolt in Hungary in 1956 had economic repercussions in Rumania no less than in the other countries of the communist world. Trade within the bloc was interrupted, production was disorganised and the rate of expansion fell. In Rumania it became apparent that many of the major targets of the second Five-Year Plan, which was due to run from 1956 to 1961, would not be reached, and it was decided at the end of 1958 that the Plan should be brought to an end in 1960 and that a new Six-Year Plan should be prepared to begin in that year. This was, incidentally, to coincide with the Soviet Six-Year Plan which was also under preparation.

It appears that it was at this time—in 1958 and 1959—that the Rumanian leaders undertook a general review of their economic policy in the light of the not inconsiderable progress they had already made and of the new situation that had developed in the communist world following the Hungarian revolt. They appear to have come to the conclusion that they could now raise their economic sights and aim at turning Rumania into a well-developed industrial nation in its own right. This objective was summarised in the phrase 'rapid and all-round industrialisation' which was to be the Rumanian communists' economic war-cry for many years to come.

This decision by the Rumanian leaders lay at the root of their later differences with the Russians and the other communist leaders who chose not to agree with them, because it cut right across the Russians' ideas of what was economically good for their east European allies. It was true that they had always subscribed to the view that industrialisation and above all the priority expansion of heavy industry was of the very essence of communism, and they had actively encouraged the communist governments to industrialise their countries. But the Russians' involvement in the expansion of their allies' industrial capacity was not entirely disinterested. They were happy to see the countries of eastern Europe developing industries for which they had natural resources or which were of value to the Soviet economy, and they saw every reason for helping the expansion of industries which would also increase a country's dependence on the Soviet Union. But they were not interested in converting every one of their dependent states into a sturdy, independent industrial nation. From the purely Russian point of view it would have made no sense to do any such thing. There was no point in every country of eastern Europe becoming a steel producer or a manufacturer of motor-cars. It was far better, from the Russian point of view, that the Poles should continue to produce their coal and perhaps some iron and steel, that the Czechs should continue to be the engineers of the bloc, that the Rumanians should go on producing oil and the oil industry equipment they knew so much about, and that the Bulgarians and the Albanians should tend their fields and their market gardens. If, as they all maintained, the 'socialist camp' was just one happy family united in communism and pursuing the same general ends, such an arrangement was surely reasonable and the least wasteful of effort. What is more, of course, it would inevitably make each of the communist countries progressively more dependent on each other and, above all, on the Soviet Union. What was wrong with that?

The Rumanian leaders saw a great deal that was wrong with this view, and their policy of 'rapid and all-round industrialisation' was their answer to it. It was in effect their proclamation that every communist country was entitled to develop whatever branch of its economy it wished in order to increase its own national wealth, without being bound by the nature of its own natural resources and the traditional structure of its economy. Moreover, in the Rumanian view, every country was entitled to expect that the Soviet government and the other communist governments would help and not hinder the achievement of such an objective.

The first sign of the Rumanian leaders' intention to speed up the rate of economic expansion was given at the meeting of the party's Central Committee in November 1958. Gheorghiu-Dej announced that the country's industrial production would have grown in 1958 by 9.5 per cent compared with 1957, instead of by the 7.9 per cent originally planned. He considered that an increase of 10 per cent was possible in 1959 and targets were set accordingly. But the actual increase in 1959 was later shown to be 11.1 per cent: practically the highest rate of growth in the whole communist bloc. Much of the increase in output was made possible through the more efficient organisation of industry rather than through the extension of capacity. Moreover, in addition to impressive increases in the output of some raw materials—notably steel, the production of which grew by 52 per cent in 1959—there was a substantial increase in the manufacture of electrical and oil equipment and in the output of the chemical industry. In short, the Rumanian economy was becoming rapidly more varied, sophisticated and efficient.

This general course of economic development was given even clearer expression in the Six-Year Plan which was finally approved at the party's Third Congress in June 1960. Gheorghiu-Dej declared with some justification that 'our country has made a giant step forward in its economic and social development' and that it had laid the foundation for further progress 'at an even higher rate'. By the end of 1960—the first year of the new plan—industrial production would be 67 per cent above the 1955 level and the engineering industry would have doubled its output in the same period, he said. There had been built 101 new enterprises and 93 new sections of enterprises, and 294 plants had been re-equipped. On the basis of these achievements, it was proposed to continue the expansion of industrial production at the rate of 13 per cent annually, so that by 1965 it would be 110 per cent above the 1959 level. Priority was still to be given to heavy industry, and in particular to the machine-building industry, which was—in Gheorghiu-Dej's words—'the fundamental prerequisite for the uninterrupted development of the national economy'. The principal products were to be oil-drilling installations, chemical and oil refinery equipment, diesel-electric engines, ships, equipment for the building industry, machine tools, trucks, tractors and other agricultural machinery. But the main single project which really signalled the Rumanians' determination to be economically independent was the iron and steel plant to be built at Galati, involving the investment of over 4,000 million lei and capable when completed of turning out some four million tons of steel a year. This plant was to be the symbol of Rumania's industrial maturity and autonomy.

However impressive the progress already made by the Rumanian economy, it was clear that the new plan could not be carried out without substantial aid from outside the country, both in the form of economic aid and in the form of more extensive trade with other countries. The rate of advance could be maintained only if Rumania could conclude large contracts (which it could hope to have at that time only from the communist world), guaranteed supplies of essential raw materials, and the up-to-date machinery that would quickly expand its industrial output. Of these, the machinery was by no means the least important, and the Rumanian economists appear to have come to the conclusion that their ends would be best served if they installed into their industry the most advanced, sophisticated and reliable machinery the world had to offer, even if it were more expensive and had to be paid for in the 'hard' currencies of the Western world.

It was for this reason that the Rumanian government took steps in 1959 and 1960 to remove obstacles to the expansion of Rumania's trade with the West. Prime Minister Stoica's remarks at the beginning of 1958 (see page 43) about Rumania's willingness to buy machinery in the United States did not bear much immediate fruit. Consequently he dropped some further hints later in the year about his government's readiness to develop trade with the countries of western Europe. But an obstacle to the development of trade with the West was the absence of any satisfactory agreement about the compensation for property lost or confiscated during and after the war. In March 1959 such an agreement was signed with the French government, and a partial agreement was reached with the British in 1960, when American claims were also settled.

Then, in the summer of 1959, a very powerful governmental delegation, headed by Alexandru Barladeanu, visited six western European capitals with the clear intention of concluding major trade deals. They appear to have spent something in the region of $100 million, including some $25 million for a motor-tyre factory from Britain, and $20 million for petro-chemical equipment from France and Italy. In 1960 Rumania's imports from western Europe increased to 22.8 per cent of its total imports compared with 15.1 per cent in 1959, and exports to western Europe rose from 16.4 per cent to 22.1 per cent. This was the beginning of a swing in the orientation of Rumania's foreign trade that was to continue and to cause friction with its communist allies.

Nevertheless Rumania's foreign trade remained at the time predominately (68 per cent) orientated towards Russia and the countries of Eastern Europe, upon which the Rumanian economy was dependent for the supply of a wide range of essential raw materials and also—particularly in the cases of East Germany and Czechoslovakia—certain engineering products. Much of Rumania's economic planning was based on the assumption that its main alliance would continue to be with the communist world. It was essential therefore for the planners to know exactly how much aid and trade they could expect from Russia during the Six-Year Plan period. It was for this purpose that Barladeanu, accompanied by a top-level team of planners and economists, spent no less than seven weeks in Moscow in the spring of 1960. The length of these negotiations suggested that there were serious differences of opinion between Russians and Rumanians, presumably on the structure of the Rumanian economic plan and the extent to which the Russians were prepared to assist Rumanian economic ambitions. Sufficient agreement appears to have been reached, however, for the Rumanians to commit themselves to their plan in the spring of 1960, although it was not until November that the two governments signed their long-term agreements in Moscow.

The Russo-Rumanian trade agreement, covering the years 1961-5, provided for a total exchange of goods between the two countries of $3.25 million—40 per cent greater than in the preceding five-year period. The Russians undertook to deliver during the five years some five hundred million dollars' worth of machinery and equipment and large quantities of raw materials, including more than 7,000,000 tons of iron ore, nearly 3,000,000 tons of coke, 950,000 tons of coking coal and 2,800,000 tons of ferrous rolled goods.

A separate technical assistance agreement covering the years 1961-8 covered the construction of the steel mill in the Galati project, an aluminium plant, a chemical fertiliser plant and electric power stations. It also spoke of Russian aid in geological prospecting and in developing the processing of 'polymetallic ores', which was thought possibly to mean that the Russians were to play some part in the production of Rumanian uranium. Rumanian technologists had already claimed in 1958 that their country would soon become 'one of the largest producers of uranium, thorium, zirconium and hafnium, which can be found in abundant quantities throughout our country'.

These agreements did not represent any sensational change in the structure or volume of trade between the two countries. Two thirds of the Russian deliveries were to consist of raw materials and semi-finished goods, while Rumanian industry had to deliver mostly finished products, of many of which the Rumanian market itself was in dire need. But the agreements were tantamount to Russian approval of the Six-Year Plan and acceptance, however reluctant, of the general lines of Rumania's economic policy.

How exactly Barladeanu succeeded in winning the Russians over and what Rumanian *quid pro quo* he offered for Russian acquiescience was never revealed. But it can scarcely have been a pure coincidence that the Soviet-Rumanian agreements were not signed until November 10, 1960: the very day on which the leaders of the world's communist parties began the conference in Moscow which was to debate the growing rift between the Russian and Chinese communists. This quarrel, which was to divide the whole communist movement and the 'socialist camp' for many years to come, had first come into the open at the congress of the Rumanian Communist Party in June 1960. Khrushchev used this congress as an occasion to rally behind him the support of the other communist leaders for what he hoped would be a quick condemnation of the Chinese. In the event, the Albanian communists openly opposed Khrushchev's action against the Chinese, and other communist leaders certainly had misgivings about the wisdom of his policy.

The immediate effect of this quarrel between the Russians and the Chinese was to make the Russians, in the second half of 1960, particularly anxious not to lose the support of any of the principal parties, especially of those in power in Europe. For the first time in the history of the communist movement, the Russians were in the position of having to canvas for support among leaders who had hitherto been obliged to take orders from them. This gave those leaders a political bargaining counter in their relations with the Russians that they had not had before, and it was a counter which the Rumanian communists, who were already beginning to loosen their ties with Moscow, were not likely to ignore. If the Albanians could make use of the division in the communist world to play the Chinese off against the Russians, could the Rumanians not do something similar— though, of course, with less impetuosity and far greater tact?

The idea of Chinese involvement in the affairs of eastern Europe was by no means far-fetched; the Chinese communists' readiness to intervene in European affairs had been already demonstrated. Shortly after the Hungarian revolt and the Polish near-revolt of 1956, Chou En-lai had visited Moscow and some of the capitals of eastern Europe and had played some part in the settlement of the situation. The Chinese even claimed that it was only at their insistence that Khrushchev had taken the decision to suppress the Hungarian revolt by force and re-establish Russian control. Chinese influence was evident later in the apparent intention of three Balkan countries—Rumania, Bulgaria and Albania—to adopt in their economics a 'Great Leap Forward' policy on the Chinese pattern, though this was later dropped. When, at the end of 1961, Khrushchev severed relations with Albania, the Albanian leaders turned to the Chinese for support, which was readily forthcoming.

If the delay in signing the Soviet-Rumanian economic agreements was due to the Russians' reluctance to underwrite a development plan which was aimed at making Rumania more independent of Russia, it seems as though their signature in

November was the price they had to pay for the certainty of Rumanian support against the Chinese. At all events, when Gheorghiu-Dej, who led the Rumanian delegation to Moscow, came to report to his party on the results of the conference, he gave no hint either of the existence of a rift in the camp or of any differences between himself and Khrushchev. He spoke only of the latter's 'brilliant speeches' and the 'high appreciation' they had won from other delegates, and he acknowledged the Soviet Communist Party to be 'the vanguard of the world communist and working-class movement'. It was a relatively small price to pay for the continuation of Soviet economic aid, the withdrawal of which at that point would have seriously disrupted Rumanian plans. The Chinese gambit could in any case be used another time if necessary.

From 1958 to 1960, when the Rumanians were busy pressing ahead with their own economic plans and their bilateral arrangements with Russia, and Khrushchev was becoming increasingly preoccupied with his quarrel with the Chinese, little progress was made with the strengthening of Comecon. The Prague meeting of the Council in December 1958 dealt with the development of the chemical industry in the whole bloc and agreed on the construction of a pipeline to carry oil from the Russian oilfields direct to Poland, Czechoslovakia, Hungary and East Germany. The Rumanians had, of course, no need of Russian oil, but they can hardly have been pleased to see the Russians making it possible for them to distribute Russian oil cheaply in the European market.

Subsequently meetings dealt with raw material supplies within the bloc, the link-up of the east European electric power network with that of the Ukraine, the state of agriculture in the member-states, and the chemical industry. Meetings in July 1960 and February 1961 discussed long-term economic planning to 1980 and the organisation of trade between the member-states for the period 1961-5. But these moves towards greater integration of the bloc do not seem to have moved beyond the paper stage or to have committed the participants very deeply. Comecon was not an effective organisation with any real authority. Indeed, Wladyslaw Gomulka, the Polish leader, said in the summer of 1960: 'In the important sector of investments there is no co-operation whatever; everyone peels his own turnip —and loses by it.'

At its twelfth session, held in Prague in December 1959, ten years after its foundation, the Council agreed on a formal constitution. This document, defining the rights and duties of the member countries and the powers and functions invested in the Council and its secretariat, should have been the means of putting some real life into the organisation. But the 'Charter' turned out to be an ambiguous and ineffective document, the provisions of which seemed to reflect a reluctance on the part of the member countries to surrender any real power to the Council as an international body or to commit themselves to accepting its discipline.

The aims of the Council were described as 'the planned development of the national economies (of the member countries), the speeding up of economic and technical progress in these countries, the raising of the level of industrialisation of the countries with less developed industry, the steady increase of labour productivity, and the furthering of the welfare of the member-peoples of Comecon'. No one, not even the Rumanians, could take exception to these objectives. Moreover, the Council proclaimed itself to be founded on the principle of the sovereign equality of all the member-states. Their co-operation through the Council was 'based on the principles of equal rights, respect for national interests, mutual advantage and comradely mutual aid'.

The Charter said that the main functions of the Council were to organise 'thorough economic and scientific-technical co-operation' among the members, prepare 'recommendations' for the co-ordination of their economic plans, and to study economic problems of common interest. It would assist member-countries to carry out joint projects in various fields 'on the basis of a consistent realisation of the international socialist division of labour and the specialisation and co-operation of production'. But the 'recommendations' of the Council were in no way binding on the members. They would be 'reported for study' to the members, who would carry them out 'according to the decisions of the governments or the competent organs of those countries in accordance with their laws'. Any member-country was entitled to 'state its position' on any questions discussed in the Council and to withhold its approval from any of its recommendation or decisions. 'The recommendations and decisions do not concern countries which have abstained on a question', the Charter said. In other words, the Council had no power whatever to enforce the will of the majority on any recalcitrant member. The Charter represented no real step forward for Comecon.

The main reason why it proved far more difficult to turn Comecon into an effective organisation than it was to create the Common Market organisation through which the countries of western Europe drew together is to be found in the vastly different stage of economic and political development in which the two groups of countries found themselves. The western European countries had all enjoyed an independent existence as sovereign states for at least several generations and some, indeed, for centuries; most of them had reached an advanced stage of industrialisation and economic development in general. The point came soon after the second world war when these countries, already brought so close together by similarity of culture, religion, political institutions and economic system, and by the development of modern communications, felt a pressing need to co-ordinate their efforts, to lower the barriers dividing nation from nation, and to surrender some of their national power to a supranational body in the interests of general progress.

But the countries of eastern Europe differed in two most important respects. They were either only just beginning to acquire a sense of national independence for the first time or just re-acquiring their identity after years of German and Russian domination. The principal concern of those leaders in eastern Europe who had any national spirit was therefore to affirm national sovereignty and not to sacrifice it once again. Secondly, all the countries of eastern Europe, even those which were more advanced industrially, had fallen sadly behind in the economic race because of the demands which had been placed on them by the Russians. The countries of eastern Europe were still largely underdeveloped nations whose attention was directed naturally in the first place to their own national economic advancement. They had little interest in schemes for international co-operation, especially if they could not be certain that these schemes were intended for *their* benefit rather than that of the great power with whom they originated. The 1950s and 1960s were not the most auspicious moment for the introduction 'from above' of a 'common market' in eastern Europe, and the Russians were not the people most likely to be able to impose it.

The most important phrase in the new Charter from the Rumanian point of view was that which referred to the 'international socialist division of labour and the specialisation and co-operation of production'. What exactly the 'international socialist division of labour' meant was not spelled out in the document and it was sufficiently vague to be acceptable to everyone. But it became apparent in the course of 1960 that there were important differences of opinion within Comecon about what the 'division of labour' implied, and in April 1960 the Rumanians set out quite clearly what their understanding of the phrase was:

> The expansion and intensification of collaboration between socialist countries do not mean that these countries should develop only those branches of industry for which they possess a raw material base or those types of production for which a professional tradition and qualified personnel exist. Collaboration between Socialist countries assures the all-round development of their economy . . . [which] presupposes above all the creation and development of the decisive branches of the economy.*

The differences of opinion appear to have remained unresolved throughout 1960 and 1961. Even at the end of 1961, when the Russians approved a new program for their party at its twenty-second Congress, their handling of the question of economic collaboration in the communist camp was still ambiguous:

> The marxist-leninist parties and the peoples of the socialist countries proceed from the fact that the successes of the world socialist system as a whole depend on the contribution and effort made by each country, and therefore consider the greatest possible development of the productive forces of their country an internationalist duty. The co-operation of the socialist countries enables each country to use its resources and develop its productive forces to the full and in the most rational manner.
>
> A new type of international division of labour is taking shape in the process of the economic, scientific and technical

* *Probleme Economice*, April 1960. Quoted by Brown in *Survey*, October 1963.

co-operation of the socialist countries, the co-ordination of their economic plans, production specialisation and co-operation.

The view that every communist country had a duty to develop its own economy to the utmost accorded entirely with the Rumanians' point of view, and they would be able to quote the Soviet party program in defence of their economic policies. But there must have been opposition to them from some direction, since Gaston-Marin, the head of Rumania's economic planning body, found it necessary to say in December 1961 that the Rumanian party had been fighting against certain advocates of the view that heavy industry should be given priority within the camp as a whole and not in each separate country and that there was no need for each country to create the 'technical and material base of socialism'. These people were distorting the ideas of specialisation and co-operation in the camp,' Gaston-Marin said.

It was during the course of 1961 that these apparently theoretical differences of opinion began to find practical expression. Despite the far-reaching economic agreements reached between Rumania and Russia in November 1960, Barladeanu had to go to Moscow for talks again in March 1961. Gheorghiu-Dej visited Poland and Czechoslovakia in April, and then headed a party and government delegation to Moscow in July. Finally, Gheorghiu-Dej led his party's delegation to the twenty-second Congress of the Soviet Communist Party in Moscow in October. There were thus plenty of occasions for the Rumanian leaders to make their views heard and to study the views of the other communist leaders.

Public statements in 1961 contained no evidence of disunity in the camp. At the Soviet twenty-second Congress, Gheorghiu-Dej approved Khrushchev's further measures to eradicate the Stalin cult in Russia (though he had himself placed a wreath on Stalin's tomb on the eve of the meeting), and he supported Khrushchev in his attitude towards the Chinese communists and the Albanians. Despite this superficial unity, however, it appears that relations between Gheorghiu-Dej and Khrushchev had already begun to deteriorate, and it was rumoured that an angry scene took place between them during the Congress. It was supposed to have been sparked off by the Rumanians' action in forcing through the complete collectivisation of their farming system in the course of 1961. This move, which was an integral part of the Rumanian economic plan, provoked Khrushchev— to the great amazement of the other communist leaders—into a remarkable criticism of the policy of collectivisation. It had not, he said, been successful in Russia and he failed to understand why the Rumanians had pressed ahead with such a policy when they had no need to do so. Why did they not follow the example of Gomulka in Poland? This unexpected criticism from a man who had boasted so long of the superiority of collectivised farming, was apparently more than Gheorghiu-Dej could take calmly, and he is said to have reacted by charging Khrushchev with having abandoned marxism. This scene was perhaps no more than another example of Khrushchev's clumsiness and lack of tact in the handling of his allies. With his own agricultural policies going wrong, he was harassed by the demands for supplies of foodstuffs from the east European leaders, and his readiness to abandon collectivisation in east Europe was just another example of his 'pragmatic' approach to the problems that beset him.

Meanwhile there were other reports of differences developing between the countries of eastern Europe. The Czechs were already said to be complaining at the Rumanians' diversion of their wealth into the pockets of west European suppliers. The Rumanians, for their part, were letting it be known that they were less than satisfied with the quality of the goods they were being sent by their Comecon partners. But it was not until the next year, 1962, that the real battle on these issues was to be joined.

With differences developing within the camp it became increasingly important for Gheorghiu-Dej to have a strong and united team at the head of affairs. In 1960 and 1961 he took steps to strengthen the leadership of party and state and stream-line the instruments of power so that he could be confident of carrying his followers with him. He had already, in June 1957, removed from the leadership of the party two men—Chisinevschi and Constantinescu—whom he regarded as potential opponents. This purge coincided almost exactly with Khrushchev's defeat of the Molotov-Malenkov 'anti-party group' in Russia and may well have been connected with it. Gheorghiu-Dej charged both men with having supported Ana Pauker and Vasile Luca and with having been blindly pro-Soviet in their views. It was also alleged that they had tried to displace Gheorghiu-Dej in the early part of 1956.

This was the last major 'purge' at the summit of the Rumanian regime. From 1957 to the present day, the composition of the group of men leading Rumanian communism has been largely unchanged. There have, however, been changes in the relative importance of individuals, of which the most striking has been the elevation of Ion Gheorghe Maurer.

Maurer had been a close friend of Gheorghiu-Dej from pre-war days and had earned the leader's gratitude by organising his release from prison camp in 1944. He held ministerial posts in the early post-war period, but was in difficulties from 1948 until 1956, during the worst of the stalinist period. In 1956 he re-emerged and travelled abroad on diplomatic missions, and in 1957 was made minister of Foreign Affairs. When Petru Groza died in 1958, Maurer was appointed head of state in his place and in the same year he was restored to full membership of the party's Central Committee. At the party congress in June 1960 he was made a member of the Politburo over the heads of four candidate members. In 1961 he replaced Chivu Stoica as prime minister.

Maurer's career suggests that he owes his advancement above all to his great ability and skill as a politician and statesman. Of middle-class origin, with a university education and—albeit his father was a member of the German minority—clearly a Rumanian nationalist, Maurer perhaps embodies more than any other Rumanian leader the policies which the regime has practised since 1956.

At the same time as Maurer became prime minister Gheorghiu-Dej was made head of state, as chairman of the newly formed State Council. He thus linked in himself the party and the state and his team was in position to face the battles ahead.

6

Rumanian Victory

Now we are confronted by the need to go further and, starting out from planning on a national scale, to go in for planning at the level of Comecon, and afterwards at the level of the socialist world system as a whole. Our aim is to build the socialist world economy as a single entity.—*N. S. Khrushchev, World Marxist Review, September 1962.*

IN 1962, Khrushchev committed himself publicly and personally to the integration of the countries of eastern Europe with the Soviet Union. The chosen instrument of his policy was Comecon. By the end of the year it was clear that his plan had failed, and its failure was in no small part due to the stubborn opposition of the Rumanians.

Khrushchev's first move was made at a meeting of the first secretaries of all the communist parties of the Comecon countries held in Moscow in June 1962. This meeting agreed on the text of a document entitled *The Basic Principles of the International Socialist Division of Labour*, which was no less ambiguous on essentials than previous statements of this kind. It also agreed on the creation of an executive committee, composed of deputy prime ministers from each of the member countries of Comecon. Agreement was unanimous on the appointment of this executive, but probably only because it was not invested with any real power. No agreement was reached on what later emerged as the Russians' real intention, which was to set up an executive body in Comecon with supranational authority, capable of imposing the will of the majority on such difficult allies as the Rumanians.

That this was the Russian intention was made quite clear by Khrushchev himself in an article which appeared in *Kommunist,* the policy journal of the Soviet Communist Party in August 1962. The aim was, he said, to make the economies of the socialist camp into a 'single entity'. In the past, Khrushchev said, the Council had lacked the necessary powers to co-ordinate national economic plans properly. But the decisions of the meeting of June 1962 would enable the work of Comecon to be completely reorganised.

The Council now had the task, he said, of 'drawing up a system which will ensure going over from bilateral to multi-lateral planning and regulation of trade and accounting between the socialist countries'. For this purpose Comecon would have to have a supranational planning authority with the power to give orders to member-governments; there would have to be joint investment projects covering the whole area; and the plans of the member-countries would have to be fully co-ordinated. It was clear that the creation of such a body would be possible only if the member-states were prepared to surrender an important element of their national sovereignty, since major decisions affecting the structure of their economies would be taken, not by the individual governments, but by the supranational body.

It is virtually certain that the Russians had tried to obtain agreement for these proposals at the Moscow meeting in June 1962 and had failed on account of Rumanian opposition. This probably accounted for the visit which Khrushchev paid to Rumania immediately after the Moscow meeting. But this typical example of the Soviet leader's personal approach to diplomacy appears to have left the Rumanians unmoved. He visited a number of Rumanian industrial enterprises (though, significantly, not the Galati site) and made many speeches in which he argued that international specialisation would benefit the socialist countries more than all-round economic development by each country. The Rumanians listened politely.

But they also took steps to ensure their capacity to resist

Russian pressure. They knew that Khrushchev would not hesitate to exert economic pressure on them if they refused to yield. He had already used this weapon with great harshness, though with no success, on the Albanian government when it refused to do his bidding. And the withdrawal of economic aid had been used more than once by the Russians in their efforts to make Marshal Tito toe the line. They would certainly use it again. Indeed, Khrushchev had hinted at it in his *Kommunist* article, where he had suggested that countries that did not accept his plan of 'international specialisation' would not benefit from the proposed common investment fund. The Rumanians were still very dependent on Russian aid and its withdrawal could gravely upset their plans.

The Rumanian leaders therefore set out to seek alternative sources of raw materials and of financial aid. Immediately following the Moscow meeting, they concluded an agreement worth some $20 million with an Austrian firm for the construction of one of the Galati furnaces. In November, another contract worth nearly $40 million, was signed with an Anglo-French consortium which was to be responsible for another section of the Galati project. In the autumn, Gheorghiu-Dej and Maurer visited Indonesia and India and obtained promises for the delivery of Indian iron ore. In these and other ways the Rumanians were insuring themselves against Russian moves to coerce them and at the same time were letting the Russians know that such pressure would be ineffective.

The quarrel which broke out at the Comecon meeting in June 1962 was not concerned only with Khrushchev's new plans for the organisation and matters of principle. The bitterest exchanges appear to have taken place over very practical issues. The Rumanians were, as we have seen, very dependent for much of the equipment they needed to carry out their Six-Year Plan on the two most advanced industrial nations in the communist bloc: East Germany and Czechoslovakia. But they had been growing increasingly discontented with the quality of the German and Czech products, with the delays in delivery and the difficulty of obtaining spare parts and efficient service. Whether these shortcomings on the part of the Czechs and Germans were simply a reflection of the generally lower quality of the output of communist industries, or whether the Rumanians' allies were sending their best goods and technicians elsewhere, or whether they were deliberately obstructing Rumania's economic plans—is not known. No doubt all three factors played a part in the relations between these communist powers. The fact was that the Rumanians were being seriously hampered in their plans, and Rumanian criticisms of their allies' goods became even more outspoken. Some of these complaints appeared in Rumanian journals.

The Czech and East Germans counterattacked with charges that the Rumanians were directing foodstuffs and foreign exchange to western Europe when they should have kept them within the communist camp, especially in view of the current shortages of food in many of the east European countries. The Rumanians' reply to this was that they were determined to equip their industries with the best machinery they could find, even if it meant buying it from the 'capitalist' world with 'hard' currencies.

The Rumanians made no secret of the fact that they found capitalist suppliers superior in practically every respect. They were under no obligation under the Comecon Charter to trade exclusively with their communist allies; indeed, both the Charter and the *Basic Principles* stressed the readiness of the communist countries to trade with anyone. Although Khrushchev had sneered at the Rumanians for 'trading on the side', it must have been difficult for him or the Czechs to argue that Rumanian industry must purchase inferior products simply because they were made by members of Comecon. In any case it was impossible to force the Rumanians to do so, since they were in the fortunate position of having valuable raw materials (oil and timber, and possibly gold and uranium) which they could dispose of in the world market to obtain the foreign currency they needed.

Rumania's east European partners were therefore not in a strong position to criticise on questions of trading policy, and the Rumanians were quick to remind their critics of some of *their* sharp practices in the past. One of the specific charges which they made at the Moscow meeting in June 1962, and which soon gained wide currency in Rumania, concerned their exchanges with Poland. The Rumanians complained that the

Poles were still selling their coal to Rumania at 1957 prices, though the world price had dropped by a third since then. On the other hand, the Rumanians pointed out, the Poles were receiving corn from Rumania at prices well below the world level. The corn was used to feed Polish pigs and enabled the Polish government to export ham and bacon to Britain and America and thus to earn considerable quantities of foreign currencies. It was difficult to catch the Rumanians out in this kind of argument, and it appears that they debated to such good effect that they secured a reduction in the prices they were paying for Polish coal.

Another score on which the Rumanians were criticised was, of course, their determination to press ahead with the Galati iron and steel plant: the symbol of their 'all-round industrialisation'. To the charge that Rumania had neither coke nor rich iron ore, the Rumanian economists replied: first, that countries like France and Italy found it economic to build such plants even though the raw materials had to be fetched a long way; and, secondly, that the Polish steel plant at Nowa Huta (a project which the Russians had backed with enthusiasm) was far less fortunately situated in every important respect than the Galati plant would be. Once again, the Rumanians were too well briefed on such issues to be much moved by the complaints of their critics.

To every charge they had a reply or a countercharge. When the Czechs complained that Rumanian meat was being sold to West Germany at a time of a meat shortage in Czechoslovakia, the Rumanians reminded the Czechs that the Rumanian textile industry could make good use of the Egyptian cotton which the Czechs obtained through barter deals with Cairo. But, the Rumanians complained, the Czechs were reselling the cotton in Europe for Western currencies, and the Rumanian government had even had to pay in those currencies for cotton that had been disposed of by the Czechs.

It was clear that, with arguments being conducted on this level, the prospects for the creation of any supranational planning authority to which the Rumanians would have to submit were very remote. The Russians do not seem to have accepted defeat at once, since Khrushchev was still talking in November 1962 of the need for a supranational planning body.

But the seventeenth Comecon session in December 1962 did not endorse his plans and was said to have ended in complete deadlock.

The impression derived from reports of the debates taking place between the Comecon members is that the Rumanians were fighting a lone battle. For various reasons, both political and economic, the other east European leaders appear to have sided with the Russians against the Rumanians, though some of the Rumanian complaints must have found an echo in other delegates' hearts. The East Germans and the Czechs were ready to accept closer integration in Comecon because they thought that it would not affect their relatively favoured position. They already had fairly sophisticated economies which the Russians were interested in developing, and they did not want to see economic aid deflected to make Rumania a competitor. The Hungarians may have had other, narrower reasons for not wishing to see Rumania forge ahead economically: it would make it easier for the Rumanian government to keep the Hungarian minority in Transylvania contented. Moreover, the Hungarian rulers were not inclined to embark on any path which smacked of resistance to Russia, having once seen where such resistance could lead. The Poles, whose economic problems are comparable in many ways with those of the Rumanians, may well have sympathised with the Rumanian attitude, even if Gomulka's devotion to Moscow prevented him from actively supporting them. Finally, the Bulgarians were in a very difficult position. With the most backward economy of any of the countries of eastern Europe, Bulgaria would stand to gain most of all from a policy of 'all-round industrialisation' on the Rumanian pattern and was in fact embarked on an economic plan which included an iron and steel plant (at Kremikovtsi) comparable with the Galati project. But Bulgaria did not have the sort of resources, either in terms of raw materials or of skilled leaders and trained technicians which would enable it to resist Russian control. The Bulgarian leaders were (and are) so deeply in debt to the Soviet Union that they had no choice but to accept the Moscow line.

Walter Ulbricht, the East German communist leader, arrived in Rumania in September 1962, accompanied by his chief economic planner, Bruno Leuschner. They were apparently entrusted with the task of putting pressure on the Rumanian leaders to accept Khrushchev's plans. They spoke publicly of the need to perfect the 'socialist division of labour' and to improve the working of Comecon. But they appear to have made little impression on their Rumanian hosts.

In January 1963, Antal Apro, the chief Hungarian delegate to Comecon, spoke of some 'unhealthy symptoms' which had appeared in the course of efforts to speed up specialisation and integration among the Comecon countries. He thought that ways would shortly be found of 'breaking down the negative trends'.

From these and other indications it is clear that the Russians maintained their pressure throughout 1962 and into 1963. But Gheorghiu-Dej made it quite clear in a speech to the Rumanian Grand National Assembly on December 29, 1962, that he had no intention of abandoning his fight for Rumania's economic advancement. After paying his tribute to the 'close co-operation' and 'fraternal support' received from Russia and to the relations of 'comradely mutual assistance' existing with the other communist countries, he claimed that the successes scored by the Rumanian economy 'prove the profoundly realistic nature of the economic policy of our party, which blends creative spirit and revolutionary enthusiasm with a thorough analysis of reality in the process of socialist construction'. The plan for the coming year was, he said, fully in accordance with the capabilities of the national economy. It provided for 'steady rates of increase in all branches' and the growth rate of 12 per cent for industrial output would be even higher than provided for in the Six-Year Plan. The increases planned for some industries were indeed startling: the electric and thermal power industries were to increase output by 21 per cent, the chemical industry by over 26 per cent, and the building materials industry by over 17 per cent. In short, the Rumanians were not lowering their targets or changing the structure of their plan. Gheorghiu-Dej's speech was in effect a gesture of defiance in the face of Khrushchev's plans.

The gravity of the crisis in Comecon and the extent of the pressure being put on the Rumanians was reflected in the frequency with which the Council met in 1963. An executive committee meeting in Moscow in February was followed by another meeting, also in Moscow, in April and an 'extraordinary session' a fortnight later in Warsaw. Then, in July, the Council held its eighteenth session in Moscow, and it was at this meeting that the conflict was finally resolved in Rumania's favour.

Though the debates in the Council remain secret, the few public statements made leave no doubt that the conflict continued to centre around the interpretation to be given to the idea of the 'international socialist division of labour'. The Rumanian leaders, for their part, took the unusual step of calling a meeting of the Central Committee of their party at the beginning of March 1963 to tell its members what had happened at the meeting of the Comecon executive committee in February and to have them formally approve the attitude taken by the Rumanian delegate, Alexandru Barladeanu. A communiqué issued after the meeting declared that the Central Committee fully agreed with the *Basic Principles* of the socialist division of labour drawn up by Comecon in June 1962, but added the important phrase: '. . . in the spirit of the principles proclaimed by the 1960 Moscow Statement—of the observance of national sovereignty, and independence, of full equality of rights, comradely mutual aid and mutual benefit.' The Moscow Statement of 1960 was, in fact, a long and ambiguous document which emerged from the acrimonious arguments between the Russians and Chinese in Moscow in 1960. As a policy statement it was a most unsatisfactory compromise between the Russian and the Chinese points of view, containing on most important issues something to please everybody. But it was still accepted as the most up-to-date and authoritative statement of principles and policy for the whole communist movement. It contained many statements which supported the Rumanian stand, and in basing their policy on it the Rumanian leaders made it very difficult for the Russians to refute their arguments.

One of the most striking features of this debate in the communist world was the superior grasp of contemporary economic problems, and especially of the problems raised by the rapid expansion of an underdeveloped economy, which the Rumanians displayed. Their arguments revealed an extremely sophisticated knowledge of modern economic thought and an ability to apply it without allowing themselves to be hindered by out-of-date concepts deriving from communist theory. While the Russians and their supporters continued to mouth phrases about 'socialism' and 'the division of labour', the Rumanians gave the impression that their economic policy and their attitude to Comecon had been evolved by well-trained economists who were fully aware of the latest developments in the non-communist world and who were largely free of dogma. One such economist was I. Rachmuth, whose article on Rumania's economic policy in *Probleme Economice* in July 1963 was the most lucid exposition of the Rumanian point of view on economic growth and of the fundamentals of Rumanian policy.

Rachmuth started from the assumption that all 'socialist' countries must achieve as quickly as possible the same level of economic development. They could not be divided into industrial and agrarian or developed and underdeveloped countries. But, he said, despite rapid progress since the 'capitalist' era, Rumania remained relatively underdeveloped. In 1960, for example, its industrial production per head of the population had been only 36 per cent of East Germany's. Rumanian industry had produced per head of the population in 1961 only 23.8 per cent as much electrical energy, 7 per cent as much coal, 39 per cent as much iron ore and 22.4 per cent as much steel as Czechoslovakia produced. Rumania's national income *per capita* in 1960 had been roughly only 45 per cent of Czechoslovakia's and East Germany's. How was this gap to be wiped out?—Rachmuth asked.

The answer was, of course, to concentrate on the expansion of heavy industry and the manufacture of the means of production, especially modern machinery. This was what the Rumanian government had done and would continue to do. It was difficult, because an underdeveloped country had to expand its production faster than the more advanced countries if it was to catch up with them, and because there were problems of expanding raw material sources and of the efficient use of the available manpower. But—and this seemed to represent the nub of the argument—the less developed countries had an important advantage: they were able to take advantage of the revolution in technical advance that was occurring in the world and to introduce into their industry immediately the very latest of modern equipment.

Automation, atomic energy, the use of cybernetics in production, the introduction of new production processes based on modern technical discoveries. . . . do not allow further use in any form of existing machinery, as was possible in the technical progress in the past.

Countries now becoming industrialised are in a very favourable position, because they are unhampered by old equipment, the discarding of which would represent a loss for the economy. . . .

The Rumanian Workers' Party uses only the most modern technological developments, for this is how we will attain the economic level of the more advanced socialist countries. The great majority of the goods produced by our machinery industry is of the same technical standard as the latest products sold on the world market. . . . All these developments demonstrate our party's systematic policy of raising our industry to the highest technical level. In 1961 capital investments in our national economy were 5.2 times higher than in 1950, while Czechoslovakia's investments had increased only 3.2 times.

This 'technological' approach to the problems of rapid economic growth made good sense, but these were not the terms in which these questions were debated among the other communist countries. The other communist leaders appeared never to have moved beyond vague generalisations about 'specialisation' and the 'unity of the socialist camp', while the Rumanians had acquired a surprising maturity of economic thought. It was significant that the basic conflict of views with the Czechs and Germans was emphasised in Rachmuth's argument, as also the basic community of interests between Rumania and Bulgaria.

The Comecon meetings in Moscow and Warsaw in April and May 1962 made no progress towards resolving the conflict; at all events there were no signs of the supranational authority's being created. So, having failed to win the Rumanians over in the debates inside Comecon, the Russians once again tried to exercise direct pressure, by sending to Bucharest a top-level party delegation headed by Nikolai Podgorny, one of the secretaries of the Soviet Communist Party and supposedly a close colleague of Khrushchev. The outside world was not allowed to know what went on in the discussions between the Russian and

Rumanian leaders: throughout their quarrel the Rumanians had maintained great discretion and had never allowed any suggestion of the bitterness of their dispute to appear in their public statements. But enough was said to make the two attitudes apparent during the Podgorny visit. Nicolae Ceausescu, one of the secretaries of the Rumanian party, invoked Lenin's authority for the view that every communist country must have a heavy industry and a well developed machine-building industry, and he spoke of the need of all these countries to bring their economies up to the same level. Podgorny repeated the Russian view that the key to the economic advance of the whole communist camp lay in the co-ordination of national economic plans and 'the specialisation and co-ordination of production'.

Podgorny's visit was the last, apparently unsuccessful, Russian attempt to make the Rumanians drop their resistance before the 'summit' meeting of Comecon leaders held in Moscow in July 1963. This meeting ended in what appeared to be complete victory for the Rumanian point of view and the defeat of Khrushchev's plans. The communiqué issued after the meeting announced that the work of co-ordinating national economic plans was to be delayed, and asserted that 'bilateral consultations carried out between Comecon countries for the purpose of reaching preliminary agreement on the development of the most important branches of national and economic ties over a prolonged period create the best possible basis for the multilateral co-ordination of plans within the framework of Comecon'. This was in effect acceptance of the views of the Rumanian economists, who had always argued in favour of bilateral deals between member-countries. The communiqué also reaffirmed the member-countries' absolute faith in the principles of 'equality, strict observance of sovereignty and mutual comradely assistance'. Apart from this clear victory on the questions of principle, the Rumanians were reported to have gained the Council's formal approval for their Galati steel plant. It was, significantly enough, an East German economic journal, *Die Wirtschaft*, which spelt out the nature of the Rumanian victory most clearly. It declared, contrary to the views it had expressed previously, that all socialist countries were entitled to go ahead with a policy of industrialisation, which meant, above all, the expansion of heavy industry. 'In each country, whatever its limitation, there are certain reserves of important raw materials for the expansion of heavy industry', the journal said. It was what the Rumanians had been saying for a long time.

It was a notable achievement on the part of the Rumanians, for it was the first time, as far as we know, that the Russians had been forced to abandon a major line of policy in the communist camp and by what could be called 'peaceful, democratic means'. To what must the Rumanian victory be attributed?

It was certainly due in part to the reasonableness of the Rumanian case and the skill and determination with which the Rumanian negotiators—above all, Alexandru Barladeanu—and economists presented it. The fact that they eventually carried the Comecon Council with them suggests that some of the other east European leaders were neither entirely unsympathetic to the Rumanian case nor especially displeased to have the Rumanians fight what was, after all, their battle too. None of the countries of eastern Europe would have gained in the long run from becoming just a part of an unwieldy economic empire directed from Moscow, which is what Khrushchev's plans would have meant.

But the Russian climb-down was also due to a multitude of other factors, of which Russia's own internal economic problems were among the most important. Khrushchev's plan to bind the east European countries irrevocably to the Soviet Union was a gesture of despair and an admission that the Russians could see no prospect of retaining the economic allegiance of their allies by other means. It was in fact an admission that they did not really believe that they could win the economic competition with the Western world, as they boasted they could, and that their east European partners would inevitably drift away through economic attraction if they were not restrained by force.

It was not only economic problems that were besetting the Russians. In the summer of 1962, the dispute between Moscow and Peking was at its height, and the 'socialist camp' and the communist movement were split in two. Moscow's authority and prestige had never been lower. Then, at the end of 1962, it suffered another heavy blow in the form of the crisis over Cuba— a costly adventure which left deep scars on the Soviet economy and seriously weakened Khrushchev's position in the Kremlin.

The Rumanians undoubtedly took all these factors into

account in planning their strategy on the Comecon front during 1963. But they relied in the end on their own resources and skill. Had they not had the courage of their convictions, the whole of eastern Europe might have found itself in a few years so inextricably tied up with Soviet economy that it would have required a major upheaval to get free. The Rumanian revolt was bloodless.

7

More Than Economics

It is the sovereign right of each socialist state to work
out, choose or change the forms and methods of
socialist construction. — *Statement of Rumanian
Communist Party, April 1964.*

THE previous chapter dealt with the situation which developed
in Comecon in 1962 and 1963 and described how the
Rumanian leaders defeated Russian efforts to turn the organisation into an instrument for the control of eastern Europe. But
the Rumanian dispute with Russia was not purely, nor in fact
primarily, a matter of economics. It was simply that Comecon
had been the best and most convenient battle-ground on which
the Rumanians could make their stand, and it was natural,
especially after June 1962, when the Russians launched their
offensive, that the Rumanians should extend their campaign to
other fields. In doing so they took skilful advantage of the
situation developing inside the communist camp and inside
Russia itself. At the same time, they took care to exploit their
own success in the dispute with Moscow to consolidate the communist regime in Rumania.

Between the summer of 1962 and the summer of 1963, the
dispute between the Russian and Chinese communists reached
its peak of intensity, and relations between Moscow and Peking

sank to their lowest point since the communist regime was established in China in 1949. The head of the Chinese delegation, Chou En-lai, had found himself obliged to walk out of the Soviet Communist Party's twenty-second congress in October 1961 because of Khrushchev's attitude to the Albanian communists, and shortly afterwards the Soviet government severed all relations with Albania. The tone of the polemics flying between Moscow and Peking became increasingly bitter and the pretence that differences were purely 'ideological' was abandoned. The Russians were openly critical of the Chinese invasion of India in the autumn of 1962, and the Chinese did not hesitate to take advantage of Khrushchev's discomfiture following the Cuban fiasco. As the exchanges became more violent in the first half of 1963, so other communist parties and leaders were inevitably drawn into the dispute and came under ever increasing pressure to declare their allegiance to Moscow or Peking. Attacks instigated by the Russians on Chinese delegates to various communist congresses conducted in public made it difficult for other communist leaders not to take sides. With the breakdown of the Sino-Soviet talks in Moscow in July 1963, the situation continued to deteriorate, the Chinese aiming their attacks with growing violence at Khrushchev himself. It became practically impossible to adopt a neutral stand between Krushchev and Mao Tse-tung or to maintain normal relations with both of them. Yet this is what Gheorghiu-Dej set out to do during this period.

Certainly until the end of 1961, the Rumanian communists had given the impression, to the outside world at least, of full support for the Russians in their conflict with the Chinese. They did not apparently support the Chinese at either of the encounters in 1960 in Bucharest or in Moscow. And they gave public endorsement to the Russians' treatment of Albania at the end of 1961. It seems likely that their support was the price they were ready to pay for the continuation of Soviet aid for Rumanian economic plans and that it was continued until the summer of 1962, when Khrushchev let it be known that he was going ahead with his plans for Comecon.

As we have seen, the Rumanian-Russian quarrel had come to a head at the Comecon meeting in June 1962, and Khrushchev had made an apparently abortive visit to Rumania in the same month. He then made his new supranational plan for Comecon public for the first time in the August number of *Kommunist*. It was no accident that the Chinese, who must have been fully informed about the current state of Rumanian-Russian relations, made their first move towards improving relations with Rumania also in August 1962.

The twenty-third of August is post-war Rumania's national day and the occasion for the exchange of greetings between Rumania and other communist states. In 1960 and 1961 the Chinese communists had devoted little attention to the Rumanian celebrations. But in 1962 their message of greetings was noticeably more enthusiastic, hailing the Rumanians' 'tremendous successes' in the economic field and the 'inviolable, eternal friendship' said to exist between the Rumanian and Chinese peoples. Then, at a reception given by the Rumanian ambassador in Peking, Marshal Chen Yi, the Chinese foreign minister, affirmed that the communist countries 'must adhere to the principles of equality, mutual benefit and fraternal mutual assistance', and that 'all marxist-leninist parties are independent and have equal rights'. He then added:

> Any action or practice contrary to these principles, any attitude of not treating others as equals or attempting to impose one's views on others is detrimental to the unity of the socialist camp and of the international communist movement. The Chinese people are glad to see that relations between China and Rumania and between the parties of the two countries have always conformed to these principles and have been developing steadily on that basis.

In the context of the dispute that was going on in the communist world at the time, this was an unmistakable advance towards the Rumanians. There was no immediate apparent response from the latter, who were still concentrating their fire on the Russians. But in December 1962 a Chinese trade delegation arrived in Bucharest.

Rumania's trade with China, like that of the other countries of eastern Europe, had declined sharply since 1960, following the Russians' curtailment of their economic relations with China. Whereas Rumania had done business worth $60 million with

China in 1959, the trade between the two countries had dropped to less than half this figure in 1961 and fell even further in 1962. In April 1963, however, the Rumanian government signed a trade protocol with the Chinese providing for an increase of 10 per cent in their trade in the current year. It was the only communist government, except the Albanian, to expand its trade with China that year.

This move was followed in May by the appearance of a Rumanian trade union delegation at the Chinese May Day celebrations and the presence of a Chinese delegation at a similar function in Bucharest. In June 1963, the two governments signed a new agreement on scientific co-operation, which was followed by the visit of a Rumanian scientific and cultural delegation to China and the conclusion of a cultural agreement. More attention was given to these exchanges in the Chinese and Rumanian press than their intrinsic importance seemed to justify. Though the actual volume of trade between Rumania and China would seem to have been of relatively little importance, it is possible that the services of Rumanian technicians and supplies of certain Rumanian raw materials, possibly including uranium, may have been of considerable value to the Chinese.

While these cautious moves were taking place between Bucharest and Peking, the Rumanian leaders also proceeded to show which way their minds were turning by adjusting their relations with Albania. At the beginning of 1962, in line with other countries of eastern Europe and under pressure from Moscow, they had withdrawn their ambassador from Tirana and severely reduced their trade with the Albanian outcasts. Now, in March 1963, the Rumanians—again, alone of all the governments of eastern Europe—sent their ambassador back to Tirana and concluded a new agreement which provided for an increase in Rumano-Albanian trade in 1963.

These gestures towards the Chinese and Albanians had an obvious political significance. But they were not irrelevant to the dispute within Comecon, where one of the most effective arguments used by the Rumanians against the Russians was to point out that the 'socialist camp' was not complete: that Comecon did not contain even all the countries that were accepted by the Russians themselves as 'socialist'. China, North Korea and North Vietnam were not members, though they had had observer status; Albania had been kicked out; Jugoslavia remained on the fringe of the organisation; and Fidel Castro had not seen fit to bring Cuba into it. Was it wise, the Rumanians argued, to try to 'integrate' the socialist camp before all the socialist countries were in it? And their argument was only strengthened if they themselves expanded their trade with China and Albania.

It was not, however, part of the Rumanian tactic at this point to switch openly to the Chinese side in the dispute with Russia. Rumania's government presumably thought that this would have been too provocative an act for the Russians to have taken as lightly as they had taken the Albanian defection. It may also have thought that there was no need for such impetuosity and that the differences between the Russians and Chinese would yet be resolved. The Bucharest communists may even have had reason, as early as the summer of 1963, to believe that Khrushchev, who was so deeply committed to his anti-Chinese policy, was losing his grip on power in the Kremlin. The Rumanian policy therefore was to avoid becoming involved with either side to the dispute while turning it to whatever advantage it might offer Rumania.

A major test of the possibility of such 'neutrality' came in June 1963 when the Chinese communists published their *Proposal Concerning the General Line of the International Communist Movement* which was a complete statement of their stand on all the issues being contested in the communist movement and a powerful challenge to Russian leadership of that movement. It was so dangerous a document from the Russian point of view that the Soviet Communist Party issued a statement saying that it would not be published in Russia and made it quite clear that it would prefer it not to be published anywhere else in the communist world. To emphasise the point the Soviet government expelled Chinese citizens from the Soviet Union for trying to distribute copies of the Chinese *Proposal*.

The reaction of the Rumanians to the Russian prohibition was to publish a lengthy summary of the Chinese document in the party newspaper *Scanteia*. No other eastern European communist party—with the exception, of course, of Albania—chose to ignore the Russians' wishes. Yet it was an act for which the Russians could hardly take any retaliatory action, since the 'socialist camp' was supposed still to exist and its 'unity' had to be defended. Who could say that the Chinese did not have a right to have their views heard?

A far more striking gesture—though, again, a perfectly legitimate one—was Gheorghiu-Dej's failure to attend the gathering in East Berlin at the end of June 1963 of east European communist leaders. This occasion was designed nominally to mark the seventieth birthday of Walter Ulbricht, the East German communist leader, But Khrushchev's intention to attend the meeting turned it into a socialist camp 'summit' meeting, and it was generally believed that it would be the occasion for rallying support for the Russian point of view against the Chinese. The Rumanians later let it be known that their failure to participate was a deliberate move to disassociate themselves from any anti-Chinese action. A few weeks later, Gheorghiu-Dej appeared at the 'summit' meeting of first secretaries in Moscow; but on that occasion it was to debate questions affecting Comecon and in the event to bring about Khrushchev's defeat.

The skill with which the Rumanian leaders could exploit the division in the communist camp—and, incidentally, the scope which there now was for manoeuvre inside the camp for those who found the domination of the big powers distasteful—was best illustrated by an article written by the Rumanian prime minister, Ion Gheorghe Maurer, for the issue of the *World Marxist Review* of November 1962. This journal, which is the only periodical of international communism, edited by a Russian and published in Prague, has rarely printed contributions of a controversial nature. But Maurer's article was an exception, though the greater part of it was quite unexceptionable from the Russian point of view, with its general approval of Khrushchevian 'peaceful coexistence', its support for the partial test-ban treaty and for the Russians' call for a cessation of Sino-Soviet polemics and a conference of world communist parties. Maurer refrained from any reference to the Chinese communists by name, though he appeared to be administering a rebuke to both Russian and Chinese in such phrases as : 'It is impermissible for one party to resort to attacks and invective against another', and 'No party is permitted to impose its own line and decisions on others, to ignore the party leadership in one country or another, to call for a change in leadership, or to support any groupings within or without the fraternal parties of other countries.'

Such criticisms were not necessarily directed against the Chinese, or at any rate against the Chinese alone. When Maurer spoke of one party's trying to change the leaders of another party and supporting factions in other parties, was he pointing the finger only at the Chinese and their attempts to unseat Khrushchev and support groups in various parties? Or had he also in mind efforts which the Russians were said to have made to bring about changes in the leadership in Bucharest, and the activities of the 'Moscow' group which had been active for so long in the Rumanian Communist Party?

Words can, of course, mean almost anything, and Maurer achieved a brilliant synthesis with a new definition of what was implied by the 'international socialist division of labour' in Comecon. It involved primarily, he said,

the co-ordination of national economic plans with a view to combining international specialisation of production with all-round development of the economy of each country and doing away with the historically conditioned discrepancies between their levels, primarily through the industrialisation of the economically relatively less developed countries; the aim is to increase production in each socialist country taken separately and in the entire socialist world system as a whole. International socialist division of labour, then, helps to eradicate the aftermath of the capitalist division of labour which fettered the productive forces of our countries and tended to perpetuate their division into advanced industrial countries and backward agrarian countries.

This was presumably the compromise formula upon which the Comecon members had agreed in July and which meant, in fact, replacing the Russian interpretation of the 'international division of labour' by a Rumanian interpretation. Or, if the Russians were inclined to argue, it was the replacement of a 'capitalist' interpretation of the idea by a 'socialist' one. The Rumanians were showing that they knew their Marx and Lenin.

The Rumanian prime minister also demonstrated his skill in walking the dialectical tight-rope when he mentioned, among the things which it was in his view 'impermissible' for one communist party to do to another, the branding 'as non-socialist a country which is socialist by the very nature of its socio-political system'. This was undoubtedly a reference to Jugoslavia and to the strong criticisms currently being made by the Chinese communists of Marshal Tito's 'revisionism'. Relations between the Chinese and Jugoslav communists had long been at the level of open and violent hostility, because, in the early stages of the Sino-Soviet dispute when neither Russians nor Chinese were criticising each other by name, the Chinese had used Jugoslav communism as the symbol of Khrushchevian 'revisionism'. This hostility had been further accentuated and perpetuated by the Chinese communists' support for the Albanian leader, Enver Hoxha, who was at daggers drawn with Marshal Tito. The relations of a communist leader with Tito were therefore an index of his attitude to the Sino-Soviet dispute, and Gheorghiu-Dej, whose relations with Tito had long been something less than friendly, might well have continued to shun the Jugoslavs in his new flirtation with the Chinese. But Maurer's brief reference to branding a country 'non-socialist' was, in the tortuous language of the communist world, a defence of Jugoslav communism against Chinese criticisms.

Indeed, the extent of the reconciliation between Gheorghiu-Dej and Tito was already apparent as Maurer's article appeared, for in November 1963 the Rumanian leader paid a nine-day visit to Jugoslavia, during which the Rumanian and Jugoslav governments concluded an agreement for the joint construction of a large hydro-electric power station at the Iron Gates on the Danube. This important project, which had been agreed in principle in the preceding June, and which was to call for the investment of $400 million, was a striking assertion by the Rumanians of their right to embark on bilateral arrangements outside the framework of Comecon. It was also an impressive demonstration of Rumanian-Jugoslav friendship and a step forward towards closer association between all the countries of the Balkans: an idea which was never far from the surface in Rumanian thinking on foreign policy.

In December 1963, speaking to the Austrian Society for Foreign Policy and International Relations, Corneliu Manescu, the Rumanian foreign minister, recalled the various efforts his government had made since 1957 to bring about 'a multilateral inter-Balkan understanding' and making the Balkans into a nuclear-free zone. The idea, he said, had been accepted by 'certain Balkan states'.

Any general understanding among the states that compose the Balkans had been made impossible in the post-war period by the fact that the area was divided by the iron curtain, with both Greece and Turkey members of NATO. When Jugoslavia was ousted from the communist bloc, Marshal Tito tried to bring together a Balkan Pact linking Greece, Turkey and Jugoslavia. But this arrangement lapsed as relations between Jugoslavia and the communist bloc again improved. Then, just as the relations between the communist and non-communist states in the Balkans began to take a turn for the better, one of the communist states— Albania—fell out of favour, so that in 1963 the prospect of any real common action and certainly of any common organisation between all the states of the Balkans still seemed remote. But Rumania's loosening of ties with Russia, its new, friendlier relations with Jugoslavia, and the establishment of normal relations between Bulgaria on the one hand and Greece and Turkey on the other all suggested that some form of Balkan association might one day be found of interest to all the countries of the area.

The Rumanian government also demonstrated its readiness to pursue its own independent line in foreign affairs, when it seemed appropriate, by its voting at the session of the General Assembly of the United Nations in the autumn of 1963. Unlike the rest of the delegations from the Soviet bloc, the Rumanian delegation voted in favour of an American-inspired proposal to establish a nuclear-free zone in Latin America and refrained from supporting a Russian-sponsored resolution on the staffing of the United Nations secretariat.

At the same time the Rumanian government continued to improve its relations, both diplomatic and commercial, with the countries of the West. At the end of 1963, agreements were reached with the British and French governments to raise the status of their diplomatic relations with Rumania to the level of embassies. This was, on the surface, a relatively minor, formal development; but it was of considerable symbolic importance for the Rumanians (as it was also for the Bulgarians and Hungarians, with whom similar agreements were later reached). For one thing, it removed an unpleasant memory of the war, because the establishment of relations at legation level instead of ambassadorial level had been a step to mark the fact that Rumania had been an enemy country in wartime. More important was the fact that the lower status of a Rumanian diplomatist in a Western capital seemed to emphasise Rumania's 'satellite' status in relation to Russia, represented everywhere by ambassadors. The gesture was a sign of Rumania's emergence as a more independent diplomatic force in the world. A similar step was taken in relations with the United States in 1964.

Rumania's closer relations with the West began to be reflected clearly in the structure of its foreign trade in 1962 and 1963. In the early post-war years the proportion of the country's trade with Russia and the countries of eastern Europe had been nearly 90 per cent (87.4 per cent in 1947). By 1960 this proportion had declined to 73 per cent, while the figures for 1962 and 1963 were 68.7 per cent and 67.9 per cent respectively. Trade with the non-communist world increased accordingly. In absolute terms, trade with the Soviet Union continued to increase; but the increase in 1963 over 1962 was only 11.4 per cent, instead of a planned increase of 16 per cent. This redirection of trade was even more apparent in the case of trade with Poland which, in 1963, fell by 1 per cent, though it had been planned to increase it by 17 per cent. At the same time, these figures are somewhat confused by the fact that Rumania's trade with China, which was planned to increase by 10 per cent in 1963, was actually more than doubled. By 1962 Rumania was conducting a higher proportion of its foreign trade with the non-communist world than any other communist country except Russia and Poland.

The various moves on so many different planes by the Rumanian leaders in their quiet revolt against Russian control were followed closely throughout the communist world, and nowhere more closely, of course, than in Rumania itself. The Rumanian people studied each step in the development of their government's policy and probably understood exactly what was going on without the need for public explanations. With their highly developed instinct for political infighting, the Rumanians did not need to have each move in the game explained to them. But neither were they disposed to react publicly to the new trends of policy: the regime under which they lived had been too severe in its discouragement of the spontaneous expression of opinions for any of them to want to anticipate their rulers' wishes.

From the end of 1962, however, the Rumanian leaders took steps to rally more active support both from the members of their party and from the population as a whole. Though they were extremely careful not to encourage the expression of the anti-Russian feelings which they knew were not far from the surface in any Rumanian, they did not fail to exploit to their own advantage, and that of their party, the fact that they were now emerging as the champions of Rumanian independence in the face of Russian chauvinism.

The most important move towards giving the party members a clearer understanding of the direction which Rumanian policy was taking, and in this way to identify the membership more closely with the leaders, was made in April 1963 at the height of the quarrel inside Comecon. After the party's Central Committee meeting in March, which ostentatiously approved the stand being taken by Barladeanu at Comecon meetings and thus demonstrated the support which the new policy had in the upper reaches of the party, meetings of basic organisations were held throughout the country. At these meetings the party members were taken into the leaders' confidence and their approval of the general line obtained. Gheorghiu-Dej knew that his resistance to Russian pressure could serve only to enhance his prestige in the party and in the country at large.

Meanwhile the party had changed somewhat in character. In the spring of 1962, the conditions of entry had been made rather easier for former members of the democratic parties and for people who had distinguished themselves in industry and agriculture. More attention was being paid to technical and political ability and less to lip-service to marxism. This tended to give the Rumanian Communist Party, which had never been overburdened with ideology, a much more national, popular character.

At the same time Gheorghiu-Dej began to make a number of quiet, discreet gestures to let the people as a whole understand the nature of his quiet revolt against the Russians and to drive home his 'Rumania first' policy. The first such move came in December 1962 in the form of a review article in the little-read

Annals of the Historical Institute of the Central Committee of the Rumanian Workers' Party. The article took to task a Soviet historian, V. Ushakov, who was the author of a book entitled *The Foreign Policy of Nazi Germany.* What upset the Rumanian reviewer of the book (which had first appeared in 1961) was the author's failure to mention the armed uprising which took place in Rumania after the arrest of Antonescu on August 23, 1944. Ushakov had thus given the impression that Rumania's liberation from fascism was entirely the work of the Red Army.

This Russian version of the Rumanian liberation had been generally accepted by the Rumanian communists in the Stalin period and had even enjoyed the endorsement of Gheorghiu-Dej. But since Stalin's death a version more favourable to Rumanian communism had been gaining ground. There can be little doubt that the article criticising the Russian historian was a deliberate device intended to provide an excuse for putting the record straight, or at least for bending it in another direction. In a speech to the Grand National Assembly at the end of December 1962, Gheorghiu-Dej himself gave the 'correct' version of the events of 1944, though without referring to Ushakov. While admitting the important part played in the Rumanian political situation by the Russian offensive of August 1944, he claimed, for the Rumanian communists—'the only active political force in the country'—the leading role in the overthrow of the Antonescu regime. Of course, Gheorghiu-Dej said:

> nobody could imagine that in those circumstances the monarchy had become 'democratic' and 'anti-fascist' overnight. But the imminent crushing of Hitler's army and the collapse of the Antonescu dictatorship forced the king and his entourage to contact the democratic forces, headed by the Rumanian Communist Party, in order to differentiate themselves from Antonescu and thus avoid sharing the inevitable doom of the military-fascist clique.

Gheorghiu-Dej made no mention of King Michael's arrest of Antonescu. Nor did he recall the Soviet government's decoration of the young king for his action. The aim of the new version of history was to minimise the part played both by the king and by the Russians and to depict the overthrow of Antonescu and the country's liberation as primarily the work of Rumanian communists and Rumanian military. At least it restored some of the credit due to the Rumanian units which, alongside the Soviet forces, had driven the Germans out of Rumania.

The Russians apparently decided that it was better not to offend Rumanian communist sensitivities, and in March 1963 another obscure historical journal, this time Russian, gave an account of 'the victory of socialism in the Rumanian People's Republic' which repeated almost word for word the version given by Gheorghiu-Dej. The Rumanian leader had, it seemed, made his point.

An important step in the 'derussification' of Rumania, particularly of Rumanian intellectual life, was the closing down by government decree in September 1963 of the Maxim Gorky Institute in Bucharest which had for fifteen years been the main centre for the study of Russian language and literature and for the training of teachers in these subjects. It had also been one of the main channels through which Russian literary—and political—influences had been brought to bear on Rumanian intellectual life. The government's decree did not abolish the Institute's functions altogether but merged them in the faculty of Slavic Languages and Literature in a new foreign language institute which was to be part of the University of Bucharest. In this way Russian was given the same status as other major modern languages. It had already ceased to be a compulsory subject in Rumanian universities and it was soon to be abolished as an obligatory subject in the schools of general education.

This was an act of more than educational significance; for a people so conscious of their nationality and so proud of the Latin origin of their language, the obligation to learn a Slav language was particularly burdensome. Most educated people in the Balkans speak more than one language; it is an obligation which falls inevitably on members of smaller nations speaking lesser-known tongues, and they naturally choose the languages of the bigger nations to which they look for leadership or protection. Alternatively, they learn reluctantly as a matter of convenience the language of the nation which happens to be oppressing them at the time.

The language of the educated classes in Rumania between the wars had been French, though many could also speak Spanish and Italian because of their similarity with Rumanian.

English and German were less widely spoken; Russian was spoken only in the eastern areas of the country. The post-war effort to make Russian the principal foreign language was a political measure signifying Russia's post-war domination of Rumanian life. But it was resented by the population as a whole and, though it is possible to force people to conform to alien rule in many ways, it is utterly impossible to force them to perform successfully the difficult intellectual feat of acquiring fluency in a foreign language. Consequently, despite the resources behind the Maxim Gorky Institute and many other organisations with similar functions, they made little impression on the younger generation of Rumanians.

I found on my visits to Rumania in 1964 that Russian is spoken by many for whom it was the language of childhood and by others, mainly technicians, who had learnt it as a means of acquiring technical knowledge at the time when the Rumanian economy was bound to the Soviet economy. But Russian is by no means the most useful language for the visitor to Rumania to have at his disposal. French or Italian, and today even English, are of far greater practical value. I had the impression that, even where officials and employees whom I met had a fluent know-ledge of Russian, they were unwilling to display it: Russian had political implications. On the other hand, when I started to speak French in a shop or an office, it was seldom that someone was not quickly produced who could carry on a conversation with me—usually a member of the older generation.

A number of other steps were taken in the latter half of 1963, which could not be described as 'anti-Russian' but which all had the same end of removing Russia and Russian from any special position in Rumanian life. Such a move was the demoli-tion of a reading room in the centre of Bucharest which was concerned with the display and distribution of Soviet material. I stood one day with a Rumanian official looking at the empty site and wondered aloud why it had been thought necessary to create such an open space in the centre of the capital. My com-panion pointed to the façade of the building now revealed behind the empty site and asked me did I not think the appearance of the theatre had been vastly improved?

In the same way, obtrusively Russian names—recalling the first flush of the post-war 'friendship'—vanished from the fronts of cinemas to be replaced by their original non-political names (by which, in many cases, they had continued to be known by the people) or by unmistakably Rumanian names. Streets named after Russian politicians, military leaders and scientists acquired overnight Rumanian or quite non-committal labels.

Many of these gestures appeared pettifogging to the Western traveller, who cares little by what names streets or cinemas are called, and the Rumanian leaders themselves doubtless realised that the changes were trifling. But they were the sort of changes that could be made without any formal declaration of policy by the leadership and without giving the Russians any reasonable cause for complaint (whatever they may have thought to themselves about the changes). At the same time, they were changes which became known to every single Rumanian city-dweller, and probably to the peasants as well, and which were understood as surface indications of deep changes in Rumanian policy.

The process of 'derussification' was not accompanied by any corresponding rapid 'westernisation', though there were in 1964 signs that the regime was preparing slowly to extend contacts with the West and to allow some Western ideas to circulate in the country. The journal, *Timpuri Noi,* which was in fact simply the Rumanian-language edition of the Soviet *New Times*—one of the Russians' main propaganda media on foreign affairs—ceased to appear in October 1963. It was replaced by a magazine called *Lumea* (The World) which was edited entirely by Rumanians and printed only in Rumanian. As its title implied, it aimed to reflect the views of the whole world, instead of only those of the communist bloc. It consisted almost entirely of translations of articles from the world's press, with a high proportion culled from the newspapers and journals of America and western Europe. The articles for publication were, of course, carefully chosen for their views, but there was no tendency to take them exclusively from the communist or 'progressive' publications in the West. For the first time in many years, educated Rumanians had the opportunity of reading and gathering some idea of the nature and variety of political thought in the West. It was at least a step forward in a country which had had a surfeit of Russian-inspired politics but which still had no easy access to Western publications.

On the other hand, Rumanians had since August 1963 been able to listen to the various broadcasts in their own language emanating from the British Broadcasting Corporation in London, the Voice of America and Radio Free Europe. All 'jamming' of these transmissions stopped in that month, so that those who wished could listen to them, safe in the knowledge that their government no longer wished to prevent them from doing so. It was another cautious opening of a window to the West, another quiet hint to the population at large, and another reduction of Russian influence.

Measures such as these, and doubtless many others of which the outside world could have no knowledge—minor changes of policy within ministries and schools and political organisations —all had the effect of stressing the 'Rumanian-ness' of the communist regime. They did not represent an abandonment of communism—at least in so far as communism meant that Rumania would continue to be ruled by one party, the Rumanian Communist Party, that the party would continue to be ruled by those then in control of it, and that the country's administration and economy would continue to be highly centralised and authoritarian. But they were an attempt to assure the Rumanian people that Rumania was no longer bound hand and foot to Russia and that henceforward Rumania's own interests, as interpreted by its communist leaders, would have first priority. For people so strongly nationalist and Russophobe as the Rumanians this was an important step forward and one which was calculated to incline them to look more favourably on the communist regime.

This confidence was reflected in some relaxation in the rulers' attitude towards those whom they regarded as their political opponents. In 1962 and 1963, the number of people held in prisons and prison camps for political offences began to be reduced and people who had been detained for their membership of the liberal and democratic parties and for opposition, real or supposed, to the communist regime began to return quietly to their homes. It was clear that the authorities were reviewing the case histories of the 'enemies of the regime' and releasing before the expiration of their sentence those whom it believed to be harmless. This process received little publicity, and it seemed that the released prisoners themselves, many of whom had spent ten years in very rigorous conditions, had little inclination to draw attention to themselves or to re-engage in political activity.

In June 1963, however, the Council of State published a decree specifically providing for the release of 2,500 political prisoners. On this occasion it was stated officially that 2,304 prisoners had been set free in 1962, 2,892 in 1963 and 464 in the first four months of 1964, and it was claimed that all the remaining prisoners would be released by August 1964, the twentieth anniversary of the liberation from fascism. At this time it was by no means unusual, even for a foreign visitor, to see a group of prisoners, worn out and bedraggled, standing in a group at a railway station. They would stare wide-eyed at the unaccustomed life around them, looking utterly lost, and then they would shuffle off in their various directions. They were a few of the victims of social change, no longer regarded as dangerous even by the sensitive communist regime.

8

'New-Type Relations'

We convey to you our cordial congratulations on the occasion...—*Gheorghiu-Dej and Maurer to Brezhnev and Kosygin on their succeeding to Khrushchev's posts in the Soviet Communist Party and Government, October 1964.*

IN 1963 the Rumanian leaders had scored a notable victory over Khrushchev on the question of the form which economic relations between communist countries should take. In 1964 their feud with the Soviet leader shifted from the economic to the political sphere: to the question of the political relations between the countries of the communist camp and in the world communist movement as a whole. The main issue was the quarrel then raging between the Russian and Chinese communists, which seemed at the beginning of 1964 to threaten the division of the communist world into two distinct groupings. While the Rumanian communists were unable, by virtue of their relative weakness, to resolve the grand schism in the communist world, their opposition to Khrushchev and the solution which he aimed to impose on that world undoubtedly contributed to the failure of his plans. At all events, Khrushchev was removed from power in October 1964 and the possibility of a solution of the problems

100

within the communist movement on the lines put forward by the Rumanian communists was once more on the cards. Gheorghiu-Dej could be forgiven if he believed—though he was far too tactful to say so out loud—that he and his colleagues had played no small part in the final downfall of the man who had tried, not without success, to lead communism safely out of the Stalin era but who had in the end found the tasks of empire too much for him.

Economic development within the communist world repeated the pattern set in 1963: the Rumanians forged ahead with their 'rapid all-round industrialisation' and particularly with the expansion of their trade relations with the West, while most of the other communist countries seemed beset with economic problems, and Comecon remained a largely ineffective organisation.

The contrast between Rumania and the other countries of eastern Europe was clearly reflected in the message with which the various communist leaders greeted the New Year. As one commentator said, they varied in tone 'from almost unmitigated gloom in Czechoslovakia, through a kind of stolid defiance in East Germany and a moderate cheerfulness in Poland and Hungary, to outright exultation in Rumania'. The main reason for the general mood of depression in the Eastern Bloc was the substantial decline in the growth-rates of most of the communist economies, all of which were committed, not merely to expansion, but to the high rates of growth which, it was claimed, the communist system alone could achieve. Yet when the results of their efforts in 1963 became available, every one of the seven member-countries of Comecon had to admit that the rate of growth of the economy had fallen. Even the Soviet economy, which had recorded a growth of industrial output of 10 per cent in 1960 and of 9.5 per cent in 1962, could claim only 8.5 per cent for 1963. The decline from 1960 to 1963 was more striking in the cases of Czechoslovakia (the most industrialised of the communist countries) which recorded a drop from 12 per cent in 1960 to − 0.4 per cent in 1963; of Poland, a fall from 11 per cent down to 5.3 per cent; of Hungary, from 11.3 per cent down to 7 per cent; and of East Germany, from 8 per cent down to 4.9 per cent. The Rumanians also recorded a decline in 1963: to 12.5 per cent, compared with 16.9 per cent in 1960 and 14.7 per cent in 1962. But their industrial output was still expanding at an average rate of over 15 per cent, appreciably higher than the 13 per cent planned for the 1960-65 period. The only other country which could claim to have maintained a growth rate of over 10 per cent was Bulgaria, and this may have been accounted for primarily by the relative backwardness of the economy (a factor which also operated in Rumania to some extent) and by the heavy investment of Soviet capital in the Bulgarian economy. The fact remained that the economies of the greater part of the communist bloc seemed to have lost their impetus, while the Rumanian economy was still enjoying a great burst of dynamism and expansion.

In a speech on February 15, 1964, to the Bucharest branch of his party, Gheorghiu-Dej said that Rumanian industrial output in 1963 was 74 per cent above the 1959 level, and he painted an impressive picture of new enterprises being built, of investments rising at the rate of 20 per cent, of 'new technology and permanently modernising production processes' and of 'the more complex utilisation of the country's natural resources to meet the various requirements of the economy and the daily needs of the population'. He was even able, unlike any other communist leader, to claim successes in the field of agriculture where, he said, despite bad weather in 1963, the output of grain had been increased and the number of livestock had risen, 'not only on state and collective farms but also on the private holdings of the collective farmers and on other peasant holdings'. Wages were rising, more goods were coming into the shops, the housing program was going ahead in towns and village, and the standard of living was moving upwards. In the year of the twentieth anniversary of its liberation, Gheorghiu-Dej said, 'socialist Rumania offers the picture of a country in permanent progress with a complex economy and flourishing culture, placed entirely at the service of the welfare of the working people'.

If this statement contained a certain element of exaggeration, it was perhaps permissible in view of the state of the other economies of the communist bloc.

Though the Rumanian leaders did not gloat in public, they made no secret of the fact that their success was due to their original and independent stand within Comecon. They now appeared to regard that dispute as a dead letter and to be content to ignore the organisation and most of its works. Throughout 1964 Comecon made little progress with the development of any of the proposed joint projects. There was much talk at the meeting in December 1963 of the Comecon executive about joint efforts in the field of chemical production, to be based on oil supplies delivered by the new 'Friendship' pipeline to eastern Europe. But little progress appears to have been made in this direction. The plan to introduce new common prices for trading within the Eastern Bloc, following the setting up of a Comecon Bank on January 1964, had to be postponed, mainly because of the lack of any common criteria for costing and price-fixing. Meanwhile the Comecon Bank remained inactive in the absence of a common currency in which the member countries could settle their balances. Following the April meeting of the executive, the Polish delegate admitted that Comecon's work was being impeded by 'the tendency to economic autarky' and that no agreement had been reached on the working out of a common investment policy. The organisation did, however, succeed in July in reaching agreement on the creation of a common freight-car pool: an entirely rational and practical measure among countries trading so much with each other and where so much space on freight trains was being wasted. But even Radio Moscow had to admit in June that there were 'certain difficulties and a considerable number of unsolved problems and contradictions in economic co-operation between the socialist countries'. This seemed to be on the whole an understatement.

At least one communist country appears to have benefited substantially from Rumania's action inside Comecon and to have turned Comecon's stagnation to immediate use. In February 1964, the Bulgarian leader, Todor Zhivkov, went to Moscow and succeeded in extracting a 300 million rouble ($333 million) credit from the Soviet government as well as promises of greater Soviet assistance for the backward Bulgarian economy. This was an interesting development, since the Russians had already contributed about a quarter of the total investments in the Bulgarian economy since the war. Moreover, a large part of Bulgarian investments in industry was taken up by the Kremikovtsi iron and steel plant project, which was the equivalent of Rumania's Galati project and was precisely the sort of undertaking that the Russians had been opposing. It looked very much as if the Bulgarians had used the Rumanian example to blackmail the Russians into increasing their aid. They were, because of the relative poverty of their resources, deprived of the possibility of striking out in the Rumanian manner. But they were already looking towards the West for increased trade, even if they had to mortgage themselves for the time being to the Russians. Though the Bulgarian leaders remained on the surface the most orthodox and the most loyal of Moscow's allies, there could be no doubt that the Rumanian example was not lost on them, as it was not lost on the other members of the disintegrating 'socialist camp'.

The Rumanians also continued to trade on a large scale with the Soviet Union and to depend very considerably on Soviet deliveries. It had never been among their plans to cut themselves off from the Soviet economy: all they had fought for was the right to trade with any country they pleased in the interests of Rumania's own advancement. Their objection was to any *exclusive* involvement with the Soviet Union. But while they maintained their business relations with Russia, they missed no opportunity of demonstrating that they intended to stand no nonsense from Moscow. At the slightest sign of anything which they could regard as a breach of the new relationship between Rumania and Russia, they reacted with great swiftness and sharpness, sometimes with rather more violence than the provocation appeared to demand.

The first incident of this kind occurred at the beginning of June 1964, in the form of a sharp exchange between two communist radio stations. On May 30 Moscow Radio put out in its Rumanian-language program a comment on the question of economic co-operation between communist countries which was an unmistakeable, if somewhat belated, attack on Rumania's stand on this question. The policy of co-operation, the radio commentator said, was opposed by 'those who say that by relying on one's own efforts one can accomplish the task of building communism more quickly than by closely uniting with the other countries'. Was it not strange, however, the commentator asked, that the same people turned to the capitalist countries for technical aid and spent large sums of foreign currency on it? This was a repetition of the charges which the Poles and Czechs had made many years previously and which the Rumanians had already firmly rejected.

They were quick to reply to the Russian attack, though labelling it simply a broadcast 'by a foreign radio station'. A commentator on Bucharest Radio on June 5 dismissed contemptuously the argument that a policy of developing to the maximum a country's own internal resources implied a desire to isolate that country from the other communist states. It was wrong, he said, to identify the criticism of certain wrong practices and ideas in Comecon with criticism of the idea of collaboration itself. But it was the charge of 'turning to the capitalists' which really raised Rumanian ire and provided the radio commentator with an opportunity to demonstrate that the Rumanians were now masters at this kind of polemic.

Which communist countries did Moscow have in mind when it spoke of trading with capitalism?—the commentator asked blandly. The Soviet Union, perhaps, which was busy expanding trade with all the main capitalist powers? Or Poland—'in whose foreign trade the capitalist countries have a share of about 40 per cent?' Or Czechoslovakia? After all, had not Khrushchev himself just declared, as prime minister of the USSR, that 'our country will continue to develop economic and commercial relations with the capitalist countries: nor have we renounced credits, if this is to our advantage'. Did the Moscow commentator agree with Khrushchev?—asked the broadcaster. The Rumanians, for their part, thought the Soviet leader's views 'completely correct'. Never before had a 'satellite' commentator demolished a Soviet statement so effectively in public.

The second incident in Rumanian-Russian relations was of a different, almost academic nature. But, again, the Rumanian reaction was anything but academic in spirit. The affair was sparked off by the appearance in a somewhat obscure bimensual review published by the University of Moscow of an article discussing the possibility of creating a single economic region in the area of the Lower Danube. It was written by a Russian scholar, Professor E. B. Valev, an authority on Bulgaria and the Lower Danube. In this article he argued, on the basis of a detailed study of the area, in favour of the creation of an 'inter-state production complex in the Lower Danube sector' made up of territory to be taken from Rumania, Bulgaria and the Soviet

Union, totalling some 150,000 square kilometres and with a population of about 12,000,000. Valev argued that such an area would have the sort of well-balanced economy which would be best capable of advancing the industry and agriculture of the region. On the purely technical plane, his arguments appeared convincing. He concluded by saying that scholars of the Danube countries 'can and must continue to participate more extensively in finding a solution of the problem of a more complex and efficient use of the Danube's resources'.

The Rumanian reply to this was to publish, in *Viata Economica,* the complete text of Valev's article, along with an uncompromising reply. The editors were obviously confident that practically every Rumanian would reject Valev's proposals out of hand as reminiscent of earlier steps to dismember Rumania. It was not difficult for *Viata Economica* to produce convincing objections to the Russian's plan. As far as purely technical considerations went, the Rumanians pointed out that Rumania would have to contribute two thirds of the territory and nearly three quarters of the population of the new region. It would also have to contribute the greater part of the raw materials. And the commentary pointed to many of the economic objections to the scheme.

But it was not the technical questions which really bothered the Rumanian leadership: it was the impertinence of the whole idea of removing a piece of Rumanian territory and attaching it to some other unit under whatever pretext and for whatever apparently good economic reasons. Rightly or wrongly, the Rumanians chose to regard the Valev plan as at least a hint that Rumania might be parcelled up under the auspices of Comecon. 'After half the territory of Rumania has been earmarked for the Lower Danube complex', they asked, 'into what other complexes would other parts of the country be drawn?' *Viata Economica* declared that the scheme, if put into effect, would 'violate Rumania's territorial integrity and dismember its unity as a nation and a state'. Nobody was going to dispose of Rumania's resources without the authority of the Rumanian government, which alone was competent to deal with the development of its economic resources. As far as Rumania was concerned, they said, 'our country will not participate in any "interstate complex" nor in any other forms of "superstate" co-operation, "socialist integration" and so forth, because these forms violate marxism-leninism, our country's national interests, the general interests of the world socialist system, and the prestige of socialism throughout the world'.

Whether or not the Rumanians were justified in reacting so sharply to something which might have been no more than the aberrations of a Russian scholar is irrelevant. In any case, as the Rumanians doubtless knew, many a Soviet kite had been flown in a relatively obscure journal. Even if Professor Valev was not speaking for the Soviet government, his article offered the Rumanian communists an excellent opportunity for demonstrating their vigour in the defence of Rumania's integrity. It was too good an opportunity to be missed, and it also served the purpose of letting the Russians know that the Rumanians meant what they had said about non-interference in their domestic affairs.

The Russian reaction was to minimise the significance of the whole affair. The Rumanians were, they said, making a mountain out of a molehill: the Soviet leaders themselves had had difficulty in finding a copy of the journal in which the Valev article had appeared. Nevertheless, the Rumanians' point was taken, and in due course the government newspaper *Izvestia* published an article criticising Valev for his ill-considered views and disassociating the Soviet government from them.

A further significant aspect of Rumanian-Russian relations in 1964 concerned the attitude to Khrushchev himself. The Rumanian leaders gave the impression from the beginning of 1964 that they identified Soviet policy, or at least the less agreeable and clumsier aspects of Soviet policy, with Khrushchev personally. In retrospect it might almost be said that they acted as though they had foreknowledge of the Soviet leader's impending downfall.

We have seen how, in 1962, Gheorghiu-Dej was reported to have been exasperated by the Khrushchev attitude to the economic problems of the Comecon countries. Moreover, the Rumanians had done nothing to endear themselves to the Soviet leader by their defeat of the plans for Comecon with which he had identified himself. There is reason to believe that relations between Gheorghiu-Dej and Khrushchev had become very cool by the end of 1963, when Khrushchev visited Rumania secretly for a 'hunting trip'. At about this period there were rumours, which the Rumanians were at no pains to deny, that Khrushchev had tried to remove Gheorghiu-Dej from the leadership of the Rumanian party.

That there was an element of personal animosity in relations between the two countries was further suggested by the fact that Gheorghiu-Dej avoided any occasion on which he might have come face to face with Khrushchev. He did not join the other communist leaders in Moscow for the celebration of Khrushchev's seventieth birthday on April 17, though he was careful to fulfil the demands of protocol by awarding the Soviet leader Rumania's highest decoration. On the eve of this occasion, when Khrushchev appeared on Soviet television to report on a visit he had made to Hungary, the Rumanians were the only people of eastern Europe not to have the benefit of this appearance on their own television receivers. Such acts tended to strengthen the impression that the Rumanian leaders were confident that Khrushchev's days as leader of the party and state in Soviet Russia were numbered, or at least that they did not think it necessary to curry favour with him.

The major problem within the communist world in 1964 was not, however, Rumania's relations with Russia but the deep rift that had developed between Russia and China. Since the abortive bilateral talks in Moscow in the summer of 1963, there had been complete deadlock in Sino-Soviet relations, and tension was growing in the communist movement with every new attack by the Chinese on the Soviet leaders and on Khrushchev personally. The Chinese were busy organising support for their policies in communist parties in every continent—not without a considerable measure of success—and they made no secret of their readiness to set up a break-away communist organisation in competition with the Russians. Meanwhile, despite the apparent toughness with which they had earlier treated the Chinese, the Russians seemed uncertain how to carry the battle with Peking to a satisfactory conclusion, and there was certainly something less than unanimity on this subject among the leaders of communism in eastern Europe.

The relevance of the Sino-Soviet dispute to eastern Europe and the anxiety which it caused among the leaders there do not appear to have derived from disagreement with the Russians' general policy towards communist China. It would appear that the Russians' reluctance to become deeply involved in building up China as an industrial and military power—an important factor in provoking the quarrel—was understood by the east European leaders. If China had become Russia's main economic burden, the other countries of the communist camp would have had short shrift. Nor is it easy to believe that the east European leaders wanted to see their countries hitched to a communist world led by the economically backward but fire-breathing Chinese. For these reasons alone, it was natural for them to back the Russians against the Chinese, as, on the whole, they had done.

Why then did those communist leaders who had preserved any independence of thought have such strong reservations about allowing the dispute between Russia and China go to its logical conclusion: a complete break between them at all levels? What had they to lose by such a development? The answer seems to be that they believed that a final split in the movement, followed by the formation of separate and rival international organisations would inevitably mean a reversion to stricter control of the east European bloc from Moscow and that it would be difficult for them to resist the arguments for such control. So long as a final division of the communist camp and the international movement was avoided and at least the illusion of world communist unity maintained, those who ruled the countries of eastern Europe were less likely to lose the greater freedom of action and room for manoeuvre which they had gained since Stalin's death. In the clearest statement published by the Rumanian party on the division in the movement, attention was drawn to 'the danger of a repetition of the methods and practices generated by the cult of the individual'—that is, by Stalin. This seemed to be the fear that lay behind the concern with which Sino-Soviet relations were followed in eastern Europe in 1964.

The Chinese communists had not been slow to see that Rumanian dissidence could be a useful instrument in their hands in the conflict with the Russians, and they had shown signs of taking advantage of it as early as 1962. Since both Chinese and Rumanians were rebels against dictation from Moscow, their views on many issues coincided. The Chinese were unquestionably supporters of the Rumanian view that every communist country had the right to develop its own economic resources in its own way. The Rumanians certainly subscribed to the Chinese view that no communist party had the right to dictate to any other communist party what its policy should be. And if there was much in the Chinese case with which the Rumanians could not agree, that was no reason why they should support Khrushchev's all-round condemnation of the Chinese. So the Rumanians quietly restored their relations with Peking and allowed their trade with China to take an upward turn.

At the beginning of 1964, however, the Rumanian leaders decided to do more than simply turn the dispute to their own advantage: they decided to try and play the role of mediator between the two great communist powers. However ambitious such a move may have appeared, it was one for which their neutral stand in the dispute and their undoubted skill as diplomatists and negotiators fitted them. Moreover, it was a task in which they had the certain, if silent, backing of many of the other communist leaders of eastern Europe. They were not, after all, so presumptuous as to believe that they could resolve the dispute between Russia and China; their aim was the more limited one of extracting the two leading communist parties from the impasse into which their hostility had led them. They wanted to prevent the division of the communist world, not to establish either the Russians or the Chinese as 'leaders' of it, nor themselves to antagonise either of them, but rather to preserve a looser arrangement and greater freedom within the camp.

Early in February 1964, the Central Committee of the Soviet Communist Party met to hear and approve a speech by Suslov, one of the senior members of the party Secretariat, on the dispute with China. The speech was a general condemnation of the Chinese; the Central Committee agreed that the time had come for an 'ideological exposure of the anti-leninist position of the leadership of the Chinese Communist Party and a decisive rebuff to their splitting activities'. This was taken to mean that Russia's leaders were planning some firm action calculated to end the Chinese opposition, though what sort of action was not clear. On the eve of their Central Committee meeting, the Russians had apparently informed the east European leaders of the substance of the Suslov speech and had told them that they were hoping to organise 'a collective rebuff by all the marxist-leninist parties' to the ideas and actions of the Chinese communists. This, the Rumanian leaders said, 'caused us great anxiety' and they immediately addressed to the Soviet Central Committee, while it was still in session, an appeal not to publish the Suslov speech. At the same time they appealed to the Chinese not to continue their polemical attacks on the Russians but to agree to a top-level meeting with the Rumanian leaders. Both the Russians and the Chinese accepted the Rumanian proposals, and the Chinese invited the Rumanians to send a delegation to Peking. The Rumanians told the other party leaders in eastern Europe what they had done and some of them ('numerous fraternal parties') welcomed the Rumanian initiative.

The Rumanian delegation to Peking was led by Ion Gheorghe Maurer, who had already emerged in 1964 as the regime's principal negotiator with the outside world on all political matters. It also included Bodnaras, Ceausescu and Stoica. On his way home Maurer called on Kim Il Sung, the North Korean communist leader, and on Khrushchev, who was on holiday in the Crimea. The excursion does not appear to have met with much success. The Rumanians themselves claimed no more than that open polemics between the Russians and Chinese had been suspended for nearly a month as a result of the Rumanian intervention. But the Chinese refused to abandon their war of words on the Russians pending new approaches, and the Russians said they would therefore have to go ahead and publish the Suslov report. They postponed this a little longer while the Rumanian leaders made a further approach to the Chinese on March 25 to issue a joint 'appeal' by them and the Russians to all communist parties. The Russians alone accepted this idea, and on March 31, the Chinese communists resumed their public press campaign against the Russians. The Suslov speech, first delivered in February, was therefore published in the Soviet press on April 3.

The Rumanians had not been able to deflect the two communist giants from their collision course. It is doubtful whether their intervention affected in any way the ultimate course of the Sino-Soviet dispute; it does not appear to have endeared the Rumanian leaders at all to the Russian rulers, and certainly not to Khrushchev himself; and it was reported that the Chinese had chosen in the end to regard the Rumanians as mere agents of

Khrushchev. On the other hand, the Maurer trip did no apparent harm to Rumanian prestige; it served to draw attention to the Rumanian leaders' independent point of view; and it may well have provided them with invaluable information, both about the attitude of the Chinese and Russians to each other and, perhaps more important, about what was happening among the leaders of the Soviet Communist Party in Moscow. At all events, nothing that they had heard or seen in Peking or Moscow persuaded them to abandon their independent line. On the contrary, Maurer's journey appeared to have convinced them of the correctness of their stand and they proceeded to say so in quite unmistakeable terms

While Khrushchev was celebrating his seventieth birthday in Moscow on April 17, 1964, Gheorghiu-Dej was presiding over an enlarged meeting of the Central Committee of the Rumanian Communist Party in Bucharest. In addition to the 110 members and candidate members of the Committee, the meeting was attended by all the members of the Rumanian government, by the heads of all the country's national institutions and political organisations, by officials from party organisations and local government bodies throughout the country, and by senior officials in the party headquarters and the civil service. Though formally a meeting of the Central Committee, it was in fact an assembly of everyone occupying a post of any political importance in the Rumanian regime. The meeting lasted a week and was clearly intended to give the maximum possible authority to the Committee's decisions.

The proceedings themselves were not published. The official communiqué said only that the meeting had heard a report on what the Maurer delegation had done and that it had approved unanimously a statement on the attitude of the Rumanian Communist Party to the situation in the world communist movement. This *Statement* was much more than a routine declaration of policy; it was clearly an important reassessment of Rumania's position in the communist world and the first formal and complete restatement of the policy of the Rumanian party and government on the principles governing foreign relations. If much that was contained in the *Statement* had been already implied in the acts of the top Rumanian leaders, the Central

Committee meeting meant that everybody who mattered in communist Rumania had been taken into the leaders' confidence in the course of the week-long session and that Rumania's 'declaration of independence' was to be the basis of policy for many years ahead. The document was given the fullest publicity in Rumania itself and was quickly translated into English, Russian, Spanish, French and German for distribution abroad.

Much of the *Statement*, which was a lengthy document of some 16,000 words, consisted of a reaffirmation of the Rumanian communists' faith in the general doctrine and aims of the communist movement: in the inevitability of the transition from capitalism to socialism, in the wrongness of Western policy, in the need for 'peaceful coexistence', and in the aims of the 'national liberation movement', and so forth. Apart from these sections, which contained little that was new, the most instructive parts of the *Statement* were those dealing with: the achievements of the Maurer mission to Peking, which have been recorded above (page 111); the attitude of the Rumanian government to Comecon, from which a long extract was quoted in the Introduction to this book (page viii-x); a statement on the form which *political* relations between communist states should take; and an appeal for an end to the Sino-Soviet dispute.

By far the most important and original of these sections for the communist world as a whole was that dealing with political relations between the communist countries, though it was the statement on Comecon which attracted most attention at the time. In the latter, the Rumanian communists reaffirmed, with more clarity and authority than previously, their main articles of faith on the question of economic relations:

—that the economic advance of each communist country depended 'first and foremost on the utilisation of each country's internal possibilities, through an intense mustering of its own forces and the maximum use of its natural resources';

—that communist countries should co-operate and help each other in economic matters only on the basis of 'fully equal rights, observance of national sovereignty and interests, mutual advantage and comradely assistance' and that the principal way in which they should co-operate was through bilateral and multilateral agreements.

—that any form of single, supranational economic planning

authority was contrary to communist principles and had 'the most serious political and economic implications';*

—that efforts should be made to bring all 'socialist' countries into Comecon, and that 'the broadest and most flexible forms and methods of co-operation be secured to attract more and more states and to facilitate their inclusion, in step with the progress of the world revolutionary process';

—that, granted the foregoing, the Rumanians were in favour of strengthening co-operation with all 'socialist' countries and of achieving an 'international division of labour';

—that such division of labour could not, however, mean that the communist countries had to isolate themselves from 'the general framework of world economic relations'; that is to say, they were still free to trade with the West.

Such was the declaration of economic independence. The Rumanians' defence of the right to every communist country to political autonomy was no less uncompromising, and it was argued with a great deal of skill.

The fact that communist parties had come to power in a number of countries posed for the first time, the Rumanian communists said, the questions of the principles on which relations between communist states should be based. This was an 'entirely new problem' for which there were no ready-made solutions. Moreover, it was complicated by the fact that the countries concerned differed widely in size and general import-ance, in their degree of economic, political and social advance-ment, and in their national and historical characteristics. The differences, the Rumanians implied, had hitherto been less significant; but now the communist countries had developed economically and politically and the communist parties had 'matured' in their capacity to work out their own domestic and foreign policies, which now had to take into account the specific problems which faced each country within the framework of the 'socialist community'. It was thus natural, the *Statement* said, for communist states to 'display initiative and to manifest them-selves actively on the international arena'. In short, the govern-ments of the Eastern Bloc, or some of them at least, were growing up and feeling their strength and had every right to stretch their limbs, and even to strike out on their own path.

* See the quotation from this section, cited above in the Introduction, page ix.

The correct principles upon which they should collaborate with each other were, of course, much the same as those which the Rumanians had defended in the case of economic relations and which had already been proclaimed, though not always observed, by the communist movement as a whole (for example, at the meeting in Moscow in 1960); that is: 'national independence and sovereignty, equal rights, mutual advantage, comradely assistance, non-interference in internal affairs, observance of territorial integrity and the principles of socialist internationalism.' These principles constituted in the Rumanian view 'the immutable law and the guarantee of the development of the entire world socialist system'.

These principles did not mean that the communist states were not to work together. They should certainly consult with each other and work out common attitudes to certain general problems. But their unity of action was not to be brought about through 'some superstate authority' laying down unique solutions. Nor was it right—and here the Rumanians echoed a charge which the Chinese had made much of—for any one state to present its own interests as 'general interests, as objective requirements of the development of the socialist system'. No one had the right to lay down new laws for the community of communist states or to try to impose their individual experience on other countries.

The Rumanian communists admitted that there were certain factors linking the 'countries of the socialist system'; they were: 'the identity of the state system, in which the working-class plays the part of the leading social force; the common fundamental interests of defending and developing the revolutionary achievements of the peoples; unity of aims in building socialism and communism, and a common marxist-leninist ideology.' But, they affirmed, there could be no unique patterns or recipes. 'Nobody can decide what is and what is not correct for other countries or parties.' 'It is up to every marxist-leninist party, and it is a sovereign right of each socialist state, to elaborate, choose or change the forms and methods of socialist construction.'

This was, the Rumanians hastened to say, not a proclamation of independence, not an attempt to disunite the communist countries, but the only hope of preserving their unity. 'The strict observance of the basic principles of the new-type relations

115

between the socialist countries is the primary requisite for the unity and cohesion of these countries and of the world socialist system performing its decisive role in the development of mankind.' This was the Rumanian program for getting rid of the 'atmosphere of distrust and tension' that dominated relations between the communist states.

It is true that the Rumanian *Statement* did not constitute a demand for complete independence for every communist state. It recognised that the communist countries had a certain community of interests or 'special relationship' deriving from the nature of their political system, though the document failed to make it clear exactly in what way their 'common marxist-leninist ideology' might limit the freedom of action of the communist governments. But its significance lay, not in the reaffirmation of a common communist purpose, but in the uncompromising assertion of the right of every communist government to decide its own policy in the light of the interests of its own people and country first and foremost. The Rumanians were in fact saying that the time was past when the Russians could presume to treat Rumania, or any other communist state, for that matter, as a 'satellite'. The fact of subscribing to communist doctrine, and even of accepting the alliance with Russia and the other communist states, was not to be taken as an abandonment of any element of a nation's sovereign rights. 'There does not and cannot exist a "parent" party and a "son-party"—parties that are "superior" and parties that are "subordinate"—but there exists the great family of communist and workers' parties, which have equal rights. No party has or can have a privileged place or can impose its line or opinions on other parties.' This was a view which was shared, oddly enough, by the 'dogmatic' Chinese as well as by the 'revisionist' Jugoslav communists. It was one to which other communist leaders in eastern Europe no doubt subscribed, even if they were reluctant to support the Rumanians publicly or to give their *Statement* much notice in their press.

The Jugoslav communists had, of course, voiced many of the sentiments now expressed by the Rumanians many years earlier, when their conflict with the Russians under Stalin had resulted in their break-away from the communist camp. But their very isolation from the other communist states inevitably forced them to concentrate their 'revisionism' on domestic affairs

116

rather than on the question of relations between communist states. It was perhaps for this reason that the Russians, even under Khrushchev, had not been over-anxious to have Jugoslavia back in the 'camp' for fear that they would do exactly what the Rumanians were now doing. The Rumanian *Statement* was the first attempt by any party within the communist world to lay down the principles governing interstate relations, and to warn the Russians against making any attempt to infringe another communist nation's sovereignty.

But, however important the Rumanian *Statement* might be in the long run in the inner councils of the communist world, it received the minimum of public notice when it appeared. The Soviet press recorded in three lines the fact that it had been published; the communist newspapers of eastern Europe which deigned to notice it drew attention only to those parts of it dealing with the Rumanians' efforts to heal the Sino-Soviet rift.

This lack of appreciation for their deliberations does not appear to have caused the Rumanian leaders much concern. They continued to act with ever increasing vigour on the principles which they had enunciated. While Khrushchev was busy pursuing his rather diffuse foreign policy, first in Hungary in April (where he reaffirmed his views on Comecon to Rumania's least friendly neighbours), then in Egypt (where his offers of Soviet aid appear to have astonished even his own colleagues), and then in Scandinavia (where he appears to have done little more than offend his hosts), and while Moscow Radio was sniping in-effectively at Rumanian policy, the Rumanians were busy putting their policy into practice, especially that part of it which said that a communist country was under no obligation to isolate itself economically from the 'capitalist' world. In May, Gheorghe Gaston-Marin, Rumania's leading economic administrator, led an important delegation to America and reached a wide measure of agreement on the expansion and liberalisation of trade between Rumania and the United States for the first time since the war. And at the end of July, Ion Gheorghe Maurer led an equally important delegation to Paris which reached agreement on the further expansion of trade with France and on the improvement of cultural and technical links with Rumania's traditional ally in western Europe. Other important trade deals were concluded with Britain and Sweden.

In May and June 1964, the Rumanians gave the impression of being little interested in what was going on in Moscow or what Khrushchev was doing. Chivu Stoica led a party delegation to Moscow at the end of May, nominally to study 'party leadership of the economy' (a subject in which the Rumanians were not apparently in need of instruction). It appeared not to have had a very warm reception. But another party delegation, led this time by Ion Gheorghe Maurer and including Emil Bodnaras, Leonte Rautu and Alexandru Barladeanu, visited Moscow at the beginning of July and appeared to be much more warmly received.

Indeed, when the events of 1964 are reviewed, it is difficult to avoid the conclusion that, at least from the time of the Maurer visit to Moscow, the tension in Rumania's relations with Russia had greatly eased and that the Rumanians had in fact won the day. It would perhaps not be too much to suggest that their contacts with the Soviet leaders had led them to believe that Khrushchev was unlikely to last long in power and that there would be an adjustment of Soviet policy which would meet Rumanian demands.

Rumanian officials were at all events full of bounding self-confidence for the remainder of 1964. It was manifest above all in their reaction to the move which appeared at first sight to aggravate the crisis in the communist world but which was probably in fact the act which finally spelt Khrushchev's downfall: the invitation issued by the Soviet Communist Party on July 30 to twenty-five other communist parties to attend a meeting in Moscow on December 15 to prepare a world conference of communist parties. Since it was already clear that the Chinese and their supporters among the twenty-five parties would not accept the Soviet invitation, its issue could lead only to a confirmation of the division in the communist world, and it seemed to place each of the twenty-five recipients in the position of having to come down on one side of the fence or the other. Of the east European parties invited, the more amenable of Moscow's, or Khrushchev's, followers—the Bulgarian, Czech, East German and Hungarian communists—accepted the invitation during August. The Rumanians and the Poles did not respond.

The Rumanians had made their position clear in their April *Statement*. They had agreed with the desirability of calling a world conference of communist parties, but only if *all* communist parties participated and only if the conference were properly prepared. Moreover they supported what was in fact the Chinese view: that there should be talks first between the Russians and Chinese at which the composition of the preparatory commission should be agreed. The Rumanian view was that 'a conference with the participation of only some of the communist and workers' parties would run counter to the cause of unity, and would lead to an aggravation of the situation, to the isolation of some of the fraternal parties and to the establishment of a split in the world communist and working-class movement'. It was difficult to dispute this view; a preparatory commission consisting only of Moscow's supporters could call together only a conference of some, even if it were a majority, of the world's communist parties.

The Rumanians did not, however, seem to be as concerned as other communist leaders at the development. On the eve of the celebration of their National Day, August 23, Rumanian ambassadors in capitals in many parts of the world gave press conferences apparently to draw attention to the fact that the occasion was the twentieth aniversary of Rumania's liberation from fascism and to underline the part played by Rumanian communists in that event. But, when questioned about his leaders' attitude to the December meeting, more than one of the ambassadors let it be understood that the Rumanian communists would not attend. At the same time, officials in Bucharest (which I visited at the time) gave the impression that they did not take the prospect of the December meeting very seriously, and said darkly that much could happen to change the situation before December.

There was a further indication that the Rumanian leaders no longer considered Khrushchev to be of importance: they did not invite him to attend the celebration of their twentieth anniversary in Bucharest, though he had attended similar occasions in other east European capitals. The Rumanian leaders deliberately down-graded the level of representation at their celebration, at the same time making their guest list representative of the whole communist camp, thus demonstrating their belief that all the countries in the camp were equal. Russians, Chinese, Jugoslavs and Albanians were all accorded the same honours and the same courtesies. The Russians were unable to upset the Rumanian excursion into communist diplomacy by sending Khrushchev to Bucharest; they sent instead Anastas Mikoyan, the elder statesman of Soviet politics who had recently been made head of the Soviet state. He was a man with vast experience in diplomacy and in dealing with difficult situations.

In the meantime Gheorghiu-Dej had gone a long way towards restoring his relations with Marshal Tito of Jugoslavia, who was his most natural ally in his efforts to loosen ties between Moscow and the capitals of eastern Europe. Tito had, after all— although for rather different reasons—done in 1948 what Gheorghiu-Dej was doing in 1964. Both were communists; both acknowledged a special relationship between communist states; both were determined to retain their own freedom of action within the communist community. But in 1948 the Rumanian communists had joined in the chorus of denunciation of Tito, and Rumania had given asylum to Jugoslav 'Cominformists'; that is, anti-Tito communists.

By the summer of 1964, however, relations between the two leaders had been restored to friendship, Gheorghiu-Dej had been entertained in Belgrade and the two countries had agreed to carry out jointly the Iron Gates project. In June the two leaders, along with their top political advisers, had met privately at Temisoara, near the Rumanian-Jugoslav border. This was shortly after Tito had had a surprise meeting with Khrushchev in Leningrad. It seems probable that the Temisoara meeting provided the two men with an opportunity of exchanging views on the state of things in the communist camp and on Khrushchev's personal position.

At the beginning of September, Gheorghiu-Dej and Tito met again when they formally initiated the works on the Iron Gates scheme. This project, which was of undoubted importance for the economies of both countries, was a demonstration of their faith in each other's goodwill, and it was also, for the Rumanians, an example of their faith in bilateral arrangements with other communist countries. But it was one of which the Russians were believed to disapprove, in view of the heavy investment involved, and one in which Comecon was invited to play no part at all. It was thought more likely that a non-Communist and non-Comecon country—Austria—might be invited to take some part in the project. The Iron Gates hydro-electric and navigation scheme is the most striking example of the 'dilution' of Comecon exclusivity.

Shortly after the meeting at the Iron Gates, it was announced that Jugoslavia had been admitted to observer status in Comecon on surprisingly advantageous terms. It appeared, indeed, that the Jugoslav government, which had long been interested in some form of association with Comecon, had at last been admitted on its own terms. In practice, the Jugoslavs were to receive all the benefits of full membership of the organisation while retaining complete freedom of action with regard to any of Comecon's decisions. Only the Rumanians' battle within the organisation had made such a development possible. Now the Rumanians had a valiant ally within the councils of Comecon.

But before the year was out an event of far greater significance for the communist world and for Rumania's position in it took place in Moscow. On October 15, 1964, it was announced that Khrushchev had ceased to be first secretary of the Soviet Communist Party and prime minister. The Khrushchev era, the era of transition from stalinism, was over and the time had come for further changes in the communist world.

9

Changes in the Communist World

> The socialist countries have become stronger economically, politically and socially, the communist parties of those countries have matured and their capacity for solving problems of domestic and foreign policy has grown.—*Statement of Rumanian Communist Party, April, 1964.*

KHRUSHCHEV'S 'resignation' from the leadership of the Soviet party and state appeared to cause the Rumanian communists neither surprise nor pain. Alone of the rulers of eastern Europe, they refrained from any comment on the changes in the Kremlin. The news seemed to take all the others by surprise, possibly because the Soviet leaders no longer had sufficient confidence in their east European allies to be able to brief them in advance even about such a major development. Khrushchev's colleagues could not be sure whether, if they took Gomulka or Kadar or Novotny into their confidence about their intention to remove their first secretary, these leaders might not take some steps to inform or aid the man in whom they had placed so much trust. So Brezhnev, Kosygin and the rest took no chances, and the result was a certain amount of confusion in the reactions from eastern Europe. Some, like the Poles, East Germans and Czechs, stepped sufficiently out of line to recall some of Khrushchev's merits and to indicate that the manner of his departure had not pleased them. The Bulgarians quietly toed the Moscow line. The Jugoslavs appeared perplexed and slightly alarmed. The Albanians were frankly delighted, though the Chinese were very cautious in their handling of the change.

The Rumanians said nothing, beyond recording the facts of the 'resignation' and the appointment of Brezhnev and Kosygin, and publishing the message of congratulation which Gheorghiu-Dej and Maurer had despatched to the new Soviet leaders as protocol demanded. The Rumanian press appeared to see no point in entering into a discussion of the real reasons for Khrushchev's removal or of the significance of the change for Soviet policy. This may have been because they believed their own party members to be sufficiently informed about Khrushchev's policies for the significance of his removal to be obvious. Or it may have been because the Rumanian leaders wished to demonstrate their strict adherence to the principle of non-interference in the affairs of other parties. It was up to the Russians to choose whom they wished to have as a first secretary or prime minister; it was no business of the Rumanians, or of the Poles or the Czechs for that matter.

Despite the Rumanians' discretion, it soon became clear that their resistance to Khrushchev's policies had played some part in his removal. Though the reasons given for it officially were simply his advanced age and declining health, it was said that it had taken Mikhail Suslov some hours to make the full indictment against the first secretary, and in due course the main headings of the indictment were 'leaked' to correspondents in Moscow. Three of these indictments were directly connected with the Rumanian campaign in Comecon: Khrushchev was charged with having disrupted the work of Comecon by trying to enforce a wrong distribution of economic functions between the member countries; he was accused of upsetting the Rumanians by the way the 'Friendship' oil pipeline was built in eastern Europe; and he was also accused of trying to impose his views on agriculture on Rumania. There were other charges relating to Khrushchev's personal behaviour which did not mention Rumania but which may well have derived in part from his relations with Gheorghiu-Dej. And there were charges relating to Khrushchev's handling of Soviet domestic policy, notably his mismanagement of agriculture and industrial administration, which, if true, would certainly have justified the Rumanians in going their own economic way without reference to Moscow. The general implication of the indictment against Khrushchev as far as the communist camp was concerned was that he had badly mishandled relations both with the Chinese and with the east European governments, and that these relations would be put on to a more reasonable and balanced footing in the future.

Because of the changes that took place in Russia's relations with its east European neighbours after Stalin's death, Khrushchev came to be regarded in the West as a more 'liberal' ruler of the Soviet empire. Even after his bloody suppression of the Hungarian revolt in 1956, he was still considered to stand for the very antithesis of stalinism in relations within the communist camp. This was by no means true.

Stalin ruled eastern Europe by brute force; that is, by means of military occupation, police terror and economic exploitation. After Stalin's death it was found impossible to rule in his manner and the worst aspects of this kind of stalinism were abolished or at least reduced in extent. But there was no indication that the Russians under Khrushchev had any intention of abandoning the main objective of Stalin's policy, which was to keep the whole of eastern Europe subservient to Soviet policy. Khrushchev abandoned some of Stalin's methods, but he did not abandon his aims. Nor did he appear ever to doubt Russia's right to dictate to the capitals of eastern Europe.

In his relations with the communist leaders of eastern Europe, Khrushchev remained every bit as much a dictator as Stalin had been; the only thing that changed was the manner in which he exerted his dictatorship. He was no longer able, as Stalin had been, to have a recalcitrant leader in Sofia or Warsaw arrested, tried and executed (though it was under his rule that Imre Nagy the Hungarian leader, was done to death). And he was steadily losing other means of enforcing his or Russia's will. But he tried to compensate for this by the sheer force of his own presence and personality, to treat Russia's east European empire as his own bailiwick and hold it together by dashing from one capital to another. One week he would be talking to Gomulka in a forest on the Polish-Russian border, the next he would be meeting Novotny in the Hradcany castle or visiting Kadar in Budapest. Alternatively, those leaders who were most dependent on him would be in Moscow seeking a further loan or some other insurance against internal opposition. Khrushchev seemed to have unlimited faith in the power of personal friendships between leaders to ensure lasting friendship between nations. His policy was to pin his faith publicly to one individual leader and then back him to the hilt. It was in fact only a variation of stalinism and one which could not possibly provide a sure basis for Russia's relations with its allies in the modern world.

It was the great merit of Gheorghiu-Dej and his advisers that they appeared to have understood long before any other of the leaders of eastern Europe (though perhaps not before the Chinese!) that Khrushchev and his policies could not last. From at least 1962 they were in active opposition to his plans for Comecon and from the middle of 1963 Gheorghiu-Dej appeared to have severed all personal relations with Khrushchev. In August 1964, on the occasion of Rumania's 'national day', he gave an impressive demonstration of his view of what relations within the communist camp should be. His reception was attended by leaders of *all* the communist countries: Russians and Albanians, Chinese and Jugoslavs and Cubans, and the Rumanian leader was equally courteous to all of them, skilfully dividing his time and attention between the Russians and the Chinese. He was thus demonstrating his acceptance of the fact that there *was* a special bond between the countries which proclaimed themselves to be communist, but that this did not give any one of those countries any special rights over the others. So long as the communist countries respected each other's rights and independence, the communist world could remain united and even grow. But Khrushchev's policy of trying to force Russia's will on the other countries was bound to split the camp. Khrushchev's defeat seemed likely therefore to be followed by a thorough overhaul of Moscow's relations with its allies and a further more sophisticated attempt to find a more lasting basis for the communist alliance.

Much had changed in Rumania by the end of 1964. If it was still easily recognisable as a communist country, and if the contrasts between life in Bucharest and life in any capital of western

Europe were still sharp, there was no doubting the improvements that had taken place in the preceding decade. The Russian 'presence' had disappeared altogether: the hotels of Bucharest, once given over entirely to Russians, were now full of business-men from western Europe and America, all eager to sell goods and conclude contracts with the Rumanian government. Down on the Black Sea coast the new hotels, built originally to provide sea and sunshine for the striving proletariat of eastern Europe, now housed as many tourists from the West as from the East, with bars and cabarets and canned music as 'decadent' as any-where on the Mediterranean. A country which had been practi-cally closed to the West since the war was now being turned into a tourist paradise, and the *Carpati* state tourist agency was busy attracting Westerners to visit King Carol's tasteless castle at Sinaia or to shoot pelican in the Danube delta. This new eager-ness to attract visitors from the West was not unconnected with the discovery that tourism was a profitable industry and one which could produce large quantities of foreign currencies with-out involving Rumania in the need to sell its goods abroad. But it was also an indication of changes taking place in the nature of the communist regime in Rumania. It would not have been possible to admit Westerners in large numbers if the tensions which had dominated life in Rumania since the war had not abated.

The process of 'destalinisation' had been slower and less sensational in Rumania than in other communist countries. This was partly because, as the Rumanian communists claimed, they had destalinised even before Stalin died. And this was true, in the sense that they had removed those leaders who were utterly committed to a policy of subservience to Moscow. But destalinis-ation in the sense of modifying the impact of the communist regime on the Rumanian people was much slower in coming. It was not until 1961, apparently, that the authorities began to release political prisoners from the prisons and camps where many of them had been held since 1948. It was not until the middle of 1964 that it was claimed that practically everyone held on political charges had been freed. But this belated act of clemency could not wipe out in the people's memory the know-ledge of the extreme harshness with which opponents of the regime had been treated.

The release of the prisoners did not necessarily mean a diminution in the role of the police in Rumanian society or in the strength of the controls which the communist party exerted over the country's intellectual life. Indeed, the more liberal attitude towards former critics may have reflected rather the strength of those controls and the efficiency of the system. It is never easy for a foreigner to understand or to feel the impact of a police regime on the population of a country or to sense the degree of fear and mutual suspicion that it engenders. My contacts with the Rumanian people and Rumanian officials in 1964 made it clear that they are still far from relaxed and that the regime still exercises a strict discipline over its officials. Even if the black days of outright police terror—of senseless arrests and punishments and brutality—are over, the memory of them doubtless lingers on as an effective sanction against any form of indiscipline.

The severity of the controls also accounted for the lack of signs of any ferment among the intellectuals, compared with the changes that had taken place in this field in practically every country of eastern Europe and even in Russia itself. Rumanian writers and artists, who were potentially as lively and creative as those of any country in Europe, appeared to have been completely silenced by the communist regime. Only in 1964 did the first relaxation become apparent, with the publication and staging of a few works which had previously been banned. If Rumanian intellectual life was going to be restored to its pre-war vigour, it looked like being a long process.

The reluctance to destalinise was presumably a result of the relatively slow progress which the regime was making towards what was nominally its major objective: the improvement of tl.e general standard of living of the whole Rumanian people. It was clearly impossible for a country so relatively underdeveloped as Rumania to pursue a policy of 'rapid and all-round industrialisation' and at the same time make any startling improvements in the people's living standards. Economic problems consequently were a major source of discontent. Until the government could register major all-round progress on this front, it presumably felt it unwise to relax controls. At the same time, substantial progress was apparent by 1964. From my own observations it was clear that the authorities had put great effort into urban

127

housing, and a good deal of new building was to be seen in the villages as well. Consumers' goods in the shops were expensive and not always of good quality, but the flow of goods was increasing. Foodstuffs appeared to be plentiful.

One useful indicator of the degree of 'affluence' achieved was the availability of the private motor-car. Until comparatively recently, the only cars in Rumania were those belonging to the state: official cars in which ministers and ministerial or party functionaries went about their business. In the last few years, the government has spent a little of its foreign currency on the purchase of a few thousand small family cars from Italy and West Germany. These cars are put on the market in Rumania at a price which represents at least two years' wages of a skilled factory worker. Yet the waiting lists of people wanting these cars are long, and it is said that Rumanians will make almost any sacrifice to save up the sum required. Those who can afford to do so are the better paid and more favoured members of society. But the state also arranges a lottery in which a certain number of cars may be won by anyone, rich or poor, and this serves as an obstacle to the emergence of an exclusive car-owning 'new class'.

This controlled admission of the private car into Rumanian life and the part it plays in the dreams of many Rumanian citizens is highly instructive of the regime's policies. Every communist government which chooses to resist Russian pressures and eventually to throw off Russian controls—especially those which initially owed much to Russian support—have to seek other sources of legitimacy, a new raison d'être. When Tito broke away from Russia he claimed to be the true interpreter of Lenin's principles and to be realising a better form of 'socialism', with a greater degree of democracy and ' workers' control '. The Rumanians make no such claim; their claim is that they are working in the best interests of Rumania and the Rumanian people and are pursuing the economic policy best calculated to raise the country's standard of living. Unlike the Jugoslavs, they appear determined to try to achieve their ends without modifying essentially the strictly authoritarian regime they have installed. Though there may be a measure of democracy within the administration and in the economy, it is probably on the technical level and does not affect the rigidity of the one-party dictatorship.

This seems to be the nature of the 'Rumanian model', which is so strikingly different from the regimes in other communist countries. The main justification for it today is that it has registered important economic successes. If the Rumanian leaders can maintain the present rate of economic growth and continue to show the same skill in their handling of relations with the outside world, it is possible that they will win a measure of genuine acceptance and approval from the Rumanian people. This in turn could give the regime the sort of confidence that could persuade it to introduce the political reforms which the people will inevitably demand sooner or later, if social conditions improve.

Whether this happens or not will also depend on the attitude of Khrushchev's successors. One of the reasons why Gheorghiu-Dej maintained so rigid a dictatorship over the people was that, without it, he could never confidently have resisted Russian pressures. Only a leader who was absolutely sure of the loyalty of his party, his police and his army, and of their capacity to control the country, could have embarked on the path of open defiance of the Soviet leader. If the threat of Russian intervention remains, then the Rumanian regime will maintain its rigour. But if Khrushchev's successors accept the Rumanian model, the Rumanian people may enjoy some considerable relaxation in the next few years.

But *if* the Soviet leaders accept the Rumanian demand— for absolute sovereignty and for 'new-type relations' between communist states and all that that implies—then this will in turn have repercussions in the other countries of eastern Europe. The Rumanian example must already have caused much heart-searching among the other communist leaders. What the Rumanians have done the Czechs could have done long before. If Gheorghiu-Dej could defy the Kremlin, should Gomulka be more timid? Much depends upon whether the Russians are willing to encourage such dangerous thoughts as these and try to find a new basis for the communist alliance. It will be a long and difficult process.

Epilogue

KHRUSHCHEV'S departure from the political scene in October 1964 was not followed immediately by any sensational changes in communist policy, either within the Soviet Union or in Soviet relations with Eastern Europe. Khrushchev's successors appeared to be concerned rather with carrying out a thorough reassessment of Russia's position in the world and in seeking ways of extracting her foreign policy from the deadlock into which it had run under Khrushchev.

The Rumanian leaders took advantage of these months to pursue the general line of policy they had evolved since 1960, quarrelling with no one and kowtowing to no one. In particular they continued the expansion of their trade with the West, and notably with America. At the end of 1964 the Rumanian government concluded an agreement with two American corporations for the construction in Rumania of a synthetic rubber plant and a catalytic petroleum cracking unit, which were estimated to cost together about 50 million US dollars. At the same time they concluded a long-term trade agreement with the French government which provided for trade between the two countries to be almost doubled by 1969. The Rumanian foreign minister, Corneliu Manescu, paid visits to America and France.

In November 1964 the chairman of the Rumanian State Planning Committee, Gheorghe Gaston-Marin, gave the first indication that his government was proposing to carry the development of economic relations with the West beyond the stage of simple trading. He told the American publisher, William Randolph Hearst Jnr., when the latter visited Bucharest, that Rumania would welcome Western 'capitalist' investment in her industry. He was reported to have said:

> 'There is no reason why American firms should not come into Rumania and work with us. We have an economic mission of eight or ten experts negotiating towards that end in New York at this moment. . . . America imports large quantities of goods from Europe. Practically everything America imports we, and you, could manufacture here in Rumania. We have all the raw materials and cheaper labour than in Western Europe.'

Gaston-Marin went on to assure the Americans that the Rumanian authorities would ensure that the joint enterprises ran efficiently and with no labour troubles, that the government would guarantee their financial stability, and that the Americans would be able to extract profits from them in dollars. Moreover, he foresaw the possibility that America and Rumania might jointly market their products in the underdeveloped parts of the world to their common benefit.

This was a surprising departure for a communist government. It was in fact the first time that any of the governments of Eastern Europe had said so unambiguously that Western 'capitalist' participation in their economies would be welcome. Even the Jugoslav government, which had been trading with America and Western Europe on a large scale for many years, had only just reached the stage of suggesting that their economy was open to private foreign investment and assistance from the Western money markets. If the sort of invitation made by the Rumanians were to be accepted by Western financiers and businessmen it would mark an important step forward in the erosion of the dividing line between 'capitalism' and 'communism'. It would be a retreat from the exclusivity of the 'socialist camp' in economic terms, and it would make it increasingly difficult to revert to the idea of turning the economies of Russia and Eastern Europe into a 'single entity'. The fact that the Rumanian leaders found it necessary to think in terms of seeking financial aid from the West seemed to confirm the impression gained by some observers in 1964 that the Rumanian government was overreaching itself somewhat in the expansion of its foreign trade. But their general optimism seemed to be fully justified by the high growth rate which the economy continued to record. Industrial output in 1964 was reported to have increased by 14 per cent compared with 1963, and this was 2 per cent more than had been planned. Increases in some sectors of the economy were as high as 23 per cent. This encouraged the planners to set the planned growth for 1965 at 13 per cent, which was at least twice the rate aimed at by any other country in Eastern Europe. Agricultural production also showed some improvement, though by no means as spectacular as that in industry.

In their relations with the other communist powers the Rumanian leaders continued their efforts to maintain strict neutrality in the dispute between the Russians and the Chinese and to avoid being embroiled in the quarrels going on in the communist movement. Gheorghiu-Dej did not see fit to go to Moscow for the celebrations of the anniversary of the Russian Revolution in November 1964, but sent the Prime Minister, Ion Gheorghe Maurer, in his place. He did, however, attend the meeting of the Political Consultative Committee of the Warsaw Pact organisation which the Russians summoned in Warsaw in January 1965. This was the first general meeting between the Russians and their East European allies following Khrushchev's deposition, and the invitation made it clear that the Russians expected representation to be on the highest level. The Rumanians complied, though Gheorghiu-Dej appeared to do no more, and to stay in Warsaw no longer, than protocol and Rumania's membership of the Warsaw Pact demanded.

The Warsaw meeting was summoned nominally to express the member-states' disapproval of any Western plans to provide western Germany with nuclear weapons or involve the west German forces in a 'multilateral force'. This the meeting quickly did, with the usual appearance of complete unanimity. But there were some indications that something less than unanimity reigned within the communist military alliance and that it might be the scene for the next reaction to Russian control of Eastern Europe.

The Warsaw Pact was signed in May 1955 by the Soviet Union and all the communist governments of Europe: Albania, Bulgaria, Czechoslovakia, Eastern Germany, Hungary, Poland and Rumania. It came into being only a few days after the formation of the Western European Union and the granting of full sovereignty to western Germany. It was regarded as, and was clearly intended to be, Russia's reply to NATO, the Western powers' military alliance.

The Pact did not in fact substantially alter the military position in Eastern Europe when it was concluded. The Russians were in any case in complete control of the military resources of their Eastern European neighbours, and the Pact did no more than give an air of legality to the Russian presence in Eastern Europe. The Pact's headquarters were established in Moscow and its combined forces were placed under the command of a single commander-in-chief, who has invariably been a Russian marshal. Each of the member-countries has representation on the Political Consultative Committee, which is the body nominally responsible for determining the policy and strategy of the alliance.

When the Russians were obliged, following the events in Poland and Hungary of 1956, to soften the impact of their rule over Eastern Europe, the Warsaw Pact began to assume more importance. The Soviet government withdrew from the capitals of Eastern Europe the many 'advisers' who had been in control of their allies' armed forces and they promised to review the question of the Soviet troops stationed in Poland, Rumania and Hungary. Henceforward Russian control was to be exerted formally through the Pact. It is technically by virtue of a joint decision of the member-states that Soviet forces are still in Germany and Hungary. The Pact serves both to co-ordinate and unify the military resources of Eastern Europe under Russian command and at the same time to ensure that no country of Eastern Europe can develop an independent military potential. It remains the Russians' one sure means of controlling their allies, and it is, significantly, the organisation which Marshal Tito has consistently refused to enter.

The Warsaw Pact is, however, an incomplete organisation,

since it has never included all the countries of the 'socialist camp': that is, all the countries ruled by communist parties, which are now said to number fourteen. There was a time, early in the life of the Pact, when it appeared as though its sponsors intended it to extend eventually to cover the whole communist world. The meeting of the Political Committee of the Pact in Moscow in May 1958 was attended by an observer from Communist China, while the meeting in February 1960 was attended by delegations with observer status, from China, North Korea, North Vietnam and Outer Mongolia. Moreover, the Chinese, for their part, made it abundantly clear that they had no desire to remain mere 'observers' of the Pact's deliberations; they wanted to play a part in the determination of policy and assist the member-states, if necessary, in the performance of their military functions. On one occasion the Chinese delegate assured the members of the Pact of his government's readiness to despatch forces to Europe to help defend the communist world if it were attacked.

The Russians, however, appear to have been rather less enthusiastic about seeing the Warsaw Pact turned into a grand Eurasian alliance in which the Chinese and their hordes would play a major role. Nor had they apparently any intention of giving China the nuclear weapons which would make her into a modern military power, or of entering into military obligations which might permit the Chinese to involve Russia in conflicts which she could not control. These were issues which lay at the root of the Sino-Soviet conflict, and it was not surprising that from 1960 the Chinese and other Asian Communist states ceased to appear at meetings of the Political Committee, which were in any case rarely held. Even the government of Outer Mongolia, which continued to look to Russia rather than to China for support, no longer sent observers to meetings of the Pact.

From 1961 there was another absentee from the meetings. The Albanian government, though still nominally enjoying the status of a full member of the Pact, ceased to be represented at its meetings. This was a further by-product of the Sino-Soviet dispute, in which the Albanian leaders chose to side with the Chinese. As a reprisal for this indiscipline the Russians, under Khrushchev's rule, broke off all relations with Albania and presumably demanded that the Albanian government should no longer be invited to Warsaw Pact meetings. There was, however, no formal announcement that Albania had been excluded from membership. The Pact thus became a closed club for Russia and her five immediate neighbours in Europe, plus Eastern Germany.

This situation cannot have failed to give rise to a certain amount of friction within the Pact, which may have explained partly the infrequency with which the members were called together. The situation was particularly difficult for the Rumanian leaders who were trying to maintain neutrality between the Chinese and the Russians. In pursuance of this policy they had not followed the Russians in cutting off all diplomatic and commercial relations with Albania, and in 1963 they even restored their representation in Tirana to ambassadorial level again and increased their trade with Albania. The Rumanians could reasonably take the view that Albania was still, even according to the Russians, a 'socialist' country and no less entitled than East Germany to military protection and economic support from her allies.

Towards the end of 1964 there were some indications that the Rumanian leaders were beginning to feel as uncomfortable within the Warsaw Pact as they had felt in Comecon. Rumanian officials began to drop hints that there might one day be changes within the Pact as well. It seemed unlikely, however, that the Rumanian leaders would go so far as to withdraw from it. This might have been far too provocative an act for the Russians to accept quietly, and it was difficult to see what immediate benefit they would derive from it. They had in any case, always acknowledged the need for a common defence policy among the communist nations.

Nevertheless the question of Albanian participation in the Pact was an issue at the Warsaw meeting of January 1965. Shortly after the meeting the Albanians revealed that the Polish government had invited them to send representatives to attend the Political Committee's session. This was obviously an attempt by Khrushchev's successors to try to restore relations with Albania and to draw the Albanian leaders away from their new attachment to communist China. Presumably acting on Chinese advice, the Albanians refused the Polish invitation, on the grounds that the harm that had been done to them could not be so easily undone, and they listed a series of far-reaching conditions for their return to the fold. They dealt at length, not only with the injustices Albania had suffered at the hands of the Russians and other member states of the Pact, but also with what they regarded as the mistakes of policy committed by the Pact under Russian direction. The main burden of their charges was that the Russians had imposed their own will on the members of the Pact, just as they had previously done in Comecon. The Albanian statement was in fact an attempt by the Chinese to fish in the troubled waters of Russia's major military alliance.

The impact of communist China on Russia and her East European allies was felt in another direction as well. The departure of Khrushchev from the scene had done nothing to reduce the antagonism between Moscow and Peking. Though Khrushchev's successors showed some signs of wishing to moderate and limit the conflict, the Chinese leaders quickly decided that Brezhnev and Kosygin were fundamentally as 'revisionist' as Khrushchev and maintained their pressure on Moscow. One of the first acts of the Russian leaders after Khrushchev's downfall was to postpone until March 1 the meeting of twenty-six communist parties which Khrushchev had summoned for December 15. This meeting was intended to make preparations for a world conference of communist parties which would, the Russians hoped, silence the Chinese and restore unity to the communist movement. But the Chinese communists and their supporters in Asia made it quite clear that they had no intention of attending even the preparatory meeting on Russian terms, and many other communist leaders, among whom the Rumanians were the most prominent, took the view that the meeting called for March 1 could only serve to make the conflict worse. This was another issue upon which it became increasingly difficult to maintain a neutral stand.

There was thus two contradictory forces at work on relations between Rumania and Russia in the early months of 1965. On the one hand the Rumanian leaders were busy developing and broadening their contacts, especially commercial contacts, with the Western world and were clearly anxious to break down the rigid barrier between Eastern and Western

Europe and to gain greater freedom of manoeuvre for themselves. On the other hand the Russian leaders were trying to restore order and discipline into their East European sphere of influence following the confusion that had been allowed to develop under Khrushchev. It was by no means certain that the Russians would be able to halt the process of disintegration that had been gathering pace since 1956 or find a new basis upon which they could hold their East European empire together.

The situation presented the Rumanian leaders with both opportunities and problems. They wanted only to be allowed to go quietly about the business of making Rumania rich and themselves secure. They had set out on a path from which it was difficult to turn back and on which they could not stand still.

Index

DATE DUE

MAR 7 '67			
MR 23 '82			
12/22/89 NEO 1:3871252			